Poiesis Review 7

Poesis Review

· *Desire & Memory* ·
Various Authors

Alternating Current Press
Boulder, Colorado

Poiesis Review No. 7
Various Authors
©2015, 2019 Alternating Current Press

All material in *Poiesis Review* No. 7 is the property of its respective creators and may not be used or reprinted in any manner without express permission from the authors or publisher, except for the quotation of short passages used inside of an article, criticism, or review. Printed in the United States of America. All rights reserved. All material in *Poiesis Review* No. 7 is printed with permission.

Alternating Current
Boulder, Colorado
alternatingcurrentarts.com

ISBN-10: 1-946580-05-8
ISBN-13: 978-1-946580-05-4
First Edition: May 2015
First Print Edition: February 2019

To begin, begin.
—William Wordsworth

Table of Contents

FICTION
He Will Return | David S. Crohn | 14
Two by Night | David S. Crohn | 56
Homo erectus | Kevin Catalano | 64
It Won't Always Be Like This | Seth Clabough | 74
Any Similarities Between the Characters in This Purely Fictional Story and Actual Individuals Are Purely Coincidental | Phill Arensberg | 88
The History of an Odradek | Moneta Goldsmith | 98
Pseudo-Aster | David S. Crohn | 106
Tatau | Jennifer Leeper | 110
The Photographer | Andrei Guruianu | 126

POETRY
My Afternoons with Dylan Thomas | Lyn Lifshin | 9
At the Board Meeting | Noel King | 10
the doll | Normal | 11
The Forgotten Man: Five Memories and the Repercussions He Avoids in the Crucible | Marie Lecrivain | 12
Spring Training | Brian C. Felder | 13
On the day Adrienne Rich died, I take a walk in the park where we used to meet for lunch | Alex Stolis | 15
As Moon and Mother Collide | Mary Melvin Geoghegan | 16
I Am Not Now, and Have Never Been | CEE | 17
At the Vietnam Veterans Memorial Wall | Victor Schwartzman | 18
Inspiration | Jared A. Carnie | 19
The Mousehouse | Kathy Gilbert | 52
Water Sports | Noel King | 53
For the Behaviorists | David L. Tickel | 54
High & Dry | J. Bradley | 55
Interstices | Kelly Jean Egan | 58
Because We Were Taught to Love | Andrei Guruianu | 59
Girls Are Cats and Guys Are Dogs | Chris Butler | 60
Barbie Reads of Louis Braille | Lyn Lifshin | 62
White Wolf | CEE | 67
Four voices at a high school graduation | Victor Schwartzman | 68
Hold On | Mary Melvin Geoghegan | 69
My Bursting-Up Diploma | Dai Akaboshi | 70

October | Jared A. Carnie | 72
My Squadron of Choice | Brian C. Felder | 73
The Holy Fight | Normal | 76
Sara's Bedsheets: A Wedding Gift | Noel King | 77
First, a Few Things Concerning the Poet | Jason Ryberg | 78
Last Night— | Dana M. Jerman | 81
Dylan Thomas' Grave Letters | David L. Tickel | 82
Serve Me the Sky with a Big Slice of Lemon | J. Bradley | 83
Along the Old Parade Routes | Andrei Guruianu | 84
Roll Call | Marie Lecrivain | 86
Violence Jo (Sax and Violins) | CEE | 91
Words made of flesh and memory | Alex Stolis | 92
Lost and Found | Chris Butler | 93
How My SUV Helped Me | Victor Schwartzman | 94
morning after halloween | Normal | 95
In a Gift of Stickers | Mary Melvin Geoghegan | 96
Yours | Jared A. Carnie | 97
Yesterday, Ma | Dai Akaboshi | 99
Jesus didn't wash his own feet | Noel King | 101
No Words Required | Brian C. Felder | 102
The Bends | J. Bradley | 103
Barbie Wonders about Buying a Coffin | Lyn Lifshin | 104
The Knock on the Door | Noel King | 108
The man on the radio says the time to believe is past | Alex Stolis | 109
Sal Mineo | David L. Tickel | 112
Something Out There | Mary Melvin Geoghegan | 113
Madame Laveau, Fortune Teller and Police Psychic, Falls off the Wagon with a
    Resounding Thud | Jason Ryberg | 114
Endeavour | Marie Lecrivain | 116
Life Partners | Victor Schwartzman | 118
softly and tenderly home: a trilogy | The Poet Spiel | 119
Story of living on a fault line | Alex Stolis | 128
Just Weeks | Lyn Lifshin | 129

FEATURED WRITER:
JONATHON ENGELS | 20

5 Miscues in Packing: Hard-Earned, Largely Ignored Advice from a Vagabond |
    21
The Bibimbap Man | 26
The Other Side of Texas | 32
10½ Lessons in Misadventure Travel | 38
On Motorcycles with Milkshakes | 45

MATTER

Cover Artist | Loui Jover, "It Feels Like Rain" | 138
Author Biographies | 132
Acknowledgments | 137
Colophon | 138

My Afternoons with Dylan Thomas

LYN LIFSHIN

It was just a blur, like you might think,
stumbling from the White Horse Tavern,
the maples already tinged with blood.
He wasn't loud; he wasn't
his voice, wasn't that poet booming
on records, all Swansea and raging.
There was no wild dying of the light.
We stopped for egg creams. He loved

them better than the cream of a woman's
thighs many say he collapsed in, took
the long-legged bait and shipwrecked,
but it was the cove of skin, the warmth,
everything unlike the dark coal mines or
the gray mist of Rhémy. I won't forget
the softness of his curls. He wasn't my
type, too fair, and he didn't work out,

his body soft as his lips. He was more
like a pet, a kitten I could let cuddle
against me. Was I a virgin? What does
that matter. Or whether he was a good
lover. When he held my cat, who
always hissed at new people, she let
him press her into his skin, as if, like
when he held me, her fur could keep

fear from spilling and staining the
rest of Wednesday.

At the Board Meeting

NOEL KING

they tell her she's no longer
effective, that her decisions are
not incisive anymore,
that her judgment is judicial
to separation and that from herein
they are appointing another
to take her place, until such
time as she can grasp
the be-all-and-end-all
like she once used to;
but, she stumbles,
tells them she cannot remember
everything, is struggling with names
as the cancer continues
to spread
heartless.

the doll

NORMAL

her lovers, like briars &
thorns
leave their mark; leave her
looking for reprieve among the
butterflies of morning.

i see her walking the streets
of my village;
queen of the dollar store,
empress of texas hot wieners,
smiling at all; cajoling
them with the
coy tease of circe.

on the whiteness of her
neck,
i can feel the bitter noose.

The Forgotten Man: Five Memories
and the Repercussions He Avoids in the Crucible

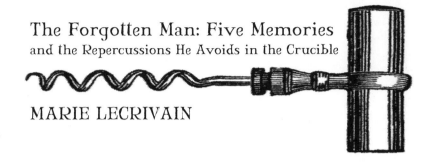

MARIE LECRIVAIN

The night Dad passed out drunk
in the middle of his son's
favorite bedtime story.
... *Ali Baba and the 40 Thieves* ...

His boyhood confession
to the priest: Grandmother beat him
with a metal hairbrush.
... *He'd hoped for more* ...

His seven nights of wet dreams
... *his little sister's succulent breasts* ...
on the eve of her 15th birthday.

The beat-up wallet he found
that contained an old man's ID,
a wedding band, and $500 in cash.
... *in a drawer ... never returned* ...

A tattoo written over the pulse
of his right wrist ... *Nullus Specialis* ...
a reward for memories
that refuse to be forgotten.

Spring Training

BRIAN C. FELDER

Coming back to the plate,
from a long winter of diversions,
I sense it's not there for me.
Not yet, anyway,
but it will be when I need it.
There's always one hit left, one poem,
in that Louisville Slugger
I call my pen; this,
something I just know as I loosen up
and take my first swing.

He Will Return

DAVID S. CROHN

We have seen how, near the end of the brief and terrible reign of Emperor Q———, the court physician said that the head of the convicted perceives everything, while the carnifex exhibits it to the crowd. This strange proclamation circulated among the people so that, in the public tumult following the emperor's own execution, a pack of his most steadfast followers absconded with his remains to a chamber off the penal courtyard. Using needle and twine, the loyalists restored head to body. They prepared his favorite supper, meat pies, elderberry wine, and a brown, tough-crusted bread, arranged a soft bed of straw for him to lie in, and awaited his reemergence. The body began to reek, and even their ardent devotion did not prevent the tracheal wound from drawing flies eager to feed and deposit eggs. After three days, one of the zealots scrupled. "The court physician is a quack," he said, and the body—now tumid and purple—should be earthed with the others in the potter's field. The loyalists thrashed him with a broomstick and cast him out. "He will return!" they cried, and let no one touch the meat pies.

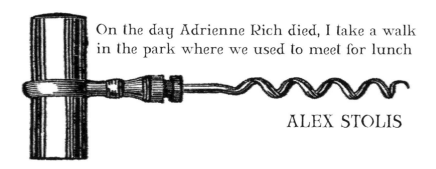

On the day Adrienne Rich died, I take a walk in the park where we used to meet for lunch

ALEX STOLIS

It's a silent movie, a sympathy fuck, a note taped to the fridge; the late-night bark of a dog that wants to be let out. It's the to

and fro of an R&B song, the back and forth of a one-sided conversation; independence from prime numbers and gravity.

There was the slow motion of uncertainty, sawdust and pool chalk; dense clouds of smoke, hiked-up skirts. It's now; it's this

piece of earth clenched in my fist. There was last call, last call, and final chances; the soft amber glow of a first crush. It is now.

As Moon and Mother Collide

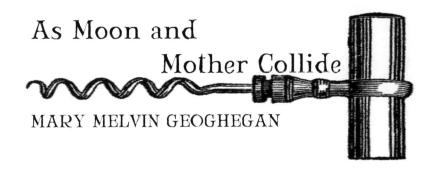

MARY MELVIN GEOGHEGAN

I take out my wedding dress
and the shoes my mother bought.
Shake out the collapsed veil
and wind it round my throat.

I release the tension in the veil
and allow it fall all over the secret,
hoping my throat will open again.
Still, guilty of something.

I Am Not Now, and Have Never Been

CEE

"From each, according to his abilities;
To each, according to his needs."

Isn't that marvelous wisdom?
But what if someone says (gleefully),
"Well ... my ability is to *sing!*"
How long before
Everyone else in the collective
Takes spades and shovels and
Bonks the crooner on the head?
How long does Stalinatra get to cry heart from the hillside,
Before he's made to dig the potatoes, too?
In our Newest Age of all-Indian-chiefs, no-Indians,
Maybe Lenny nailed it again, in that
(paraquoted) "Waiters / waitresses are the last to be liberated"
The Final Collective
To make the potatoes (or the doughnuts)
Adjusting their May 4th smiles
As we, the rest of us
Search for our very own Special Ability we just know would make
Others
So happy

At the Vietnam Veterans Memorial Wall

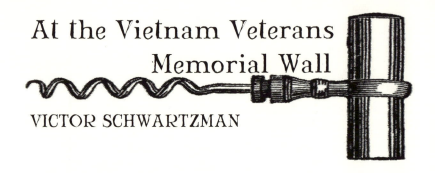

VICTOR SCHWARTZMAN

Haunted for years, I went to the Wall,
A war resister facing soldiers who died
Looking at the Wall, my crying eyes
Reflected with all those foregone lives
They made the sacrifice I refused
What sacrifice should I have made?
If it was right, why do I feel guilty?

I stood there a long time looking
All those names, some guys I knew
Someone crying; my eyes are dry
Coming home was worse than the war
Lifelong friends, though I have nightmares
Greatest time of my life and the worst
May never know if it was worth it

Never knew what hit me (land mine)
Never knew what I died for (politics)
Drafted out of my life into death
I owed my country and what a payback

Inspiration

JARED A. CARNIE

I put it on the big speakers.
The man tells me
We are all from stars
We are conscious coincidental dust
We are the universe experiencing itself
We are a miracle.

I bend down
To collect the pile
My puppy has left me
In the middle of the kitchen floor.

As I reach for it
My knee lands
In a small warm puddle
I hadn't seen
And I feel the miracle soaking through.

Featured Writer

JONATHON ENGELS

Jonathon Engels began his writing career as a lovesick poet of 12 years old, and despite his rhyming confessions of yearning failing to produce any results, he dimwittedly decided to continue with the written word. After years of working hard to hone his craft(iness), years which included many more attempts at love poetry, as well as jaunts through undergraduate (the Jim Morrison years) and graduate school (the William Carlos Williams / beatnik saga), he decided he'd be better off teaching, where he would be in control of whatever critical acclaim was being dished out. The decision to tuck tail and run has proven to have made all the difference.

At the completion of an MFA degree in Creative Writing, he packed up his belongings and moved to Korea to teach English. (Some suspect this was in an effort to insure he would be the most proficient writer of English around.) To some degree, the plan worked, and he embarked on a long (2005-2013 RIP) and wavering career on the EFL circuit, living and working in such places as Guatemala, Turkey, the Palestinian West Bank, and Russia. In Russia, where the winters were harsh and the apartment was insulated, he decided to start recounting the tales of misadventure that had found him shivering next to a radiator in Moscow. He declared himself a travel writer.

To make a long bio short, what started off as a likely unfulfilling and lonely future penning Hallmark cards turned into some seriously low-wage work writing Internet travel articles. Through a pursuit in backpacking cheaply for long periods of time, Jonathon developed an interest in permaculture (via volunteering on farms), and through Jonathan Safran Foer's haunting book, *Eating Animals*, he also found himself a converted and colluding vegan. Nowadays, he divides his devotional writing between the three subjects as a staff writer for several different websites, including *Transitions Abroad*, *Green Global Travel*, *Permaculture News*, and *One Green Planet*. Otherwise, he has spent the past few years as a happily married but somewhat homeless drifter.

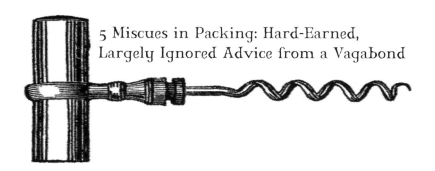

5 Miscues in Packing: Hard-Earned, Largely Ignored Advice from a Vagabond

Something about going to a new country makes me think of every inconceivable thing I might need if, say, the climate were to shift from snowing to sweltering in seconds, in a place so remote that T-shirts were unavailable, that no shirt would be unthinkable, leaving me so unprepared that … I'm not sure what I think would happen. I guess global warming has most of us fairly concerned these days. Because I travel, packing has been my major defense against it, and everything—important things like boredom, a failing memory, foul odors.

As a child, "traveling" meant the family van, shooting to Houston for a couple of Astros games, some rollercoasters, or to Gulf Shores for some sand and surf. We had a massive vehicle to fill, which we did, with household items ranging from pillows to VHS collections (it was a different time) to my stepmother's Peki-poo, a half-Pekinese / half-poodle princess with a standing weekly appointment at a "beauty shop." Picture a more middle-class version of the Beverly Hillbillies. We packed as if moving across the country as opposed to going five hours away for a week.

After leaving home for college, I learned to live leaner. As a bachelor, I adapted to one-room apartments (the size of that family van) and, on more than one occasion, slept on the floor beneath a Mexican blanket bought for two dollars in Tijuana, never once washed. I had camping equipment for furniture (and camping), "recycled" plastic dishware and utensils, and cleverly utilized packing boxes for nightstands, coffee tables, end tables, armoires, entertainment centers, and DVD cases. Left to my own bank account, I became a university student, which actually carries with it a completely different notion of *free*-thinking.

Lesson #1: Improvisation

Little did I know that college education was so much more than academic. I was unwittingly preparing myself for a life of backpackerdom and a complete rejection of anything resembling a stable career. It was from these cardboard boxes and reused fast-food cutlery that the first inklings of using things unconventionally, hobo-ish even, became second nature. It was a skill that would lie inside me, dormant until needed.

One can't predict every need that will arise, but we can improvise. For example, in Thailand, I discovered one can use a sarong for warmth, drying purposes, protection from the sun, a picnic blanket, a scarf, a tablecloth, and a wall hanging in a dingy dorm room. It isn't necessary, as once believed, to bring all the convenience of home. There are ways to match wills, stores to solve the rest. Survival doesn't require a van. Bring a Swiss Army knife—forget about it.

Occasionally, though, something from my past takes back over, and I act like a spoiled Peki-poo with bows in my hair. (There were five boys: my stepmother really could've used a daughter.) Suddenly, I need shoes for hiking, beaching, walking, running, snow trekking, underwater diving, boat decks, rain, nice restaurants, comfortable bus / train / plane rides. A new call for extras of toothpaste, deodorant, underpants, and bath towels arises. I discover there's no room left in my backpack for clothes.

I remember my third night living in Memphis, having moved there for graduate school without applying for graduate school. I was entirely at ease soaked in three days of stink because I hadn't brought a bath towel with me and couldn't find a store in which to buy one. I know I have poured water into a tube of toothpaste, getting those last dregs for a few days more of use. I've gone years, three or four, without replacing underwear. In high school, I'd steal sweaty P.E. outfits from lockers when on away games, sometimes without washing them before using them. I'm comfortable being nasty.

However, something—I think it's Southern-ness—makes me believe, even after years of experience to the contrary, other countries will not have things: clothing for fully grown men, toiletries, books. I forget having worn the same T-shirt for a week, how two of the four shelves on my bookcase remain unread. A new location seems to equate to a new person and a possible lack of resources. I pack like my father would, unwilling to do without anything. Then, as my trip progresses, I begin to shed the fluff, leaving a trail of personal artifacts behind me.

Lesson #2: Books and the Toilet

One book: Not only can it be read more than once (just like watching a movie multiple times), but there are book swaps at most hostels, or other travelers willing to trade their books. As well, if you speak English, which if you've made it this far into this article is highly likely, then books are available ... everywhere. Like me, of a certain age and tax bracket, there are still many who haven't gone the way of the Kindle. After carrying books around for a bit, realizing the read wasn't worth the weight, I'm fairly sure I have begun libraries in remote parts of the world.

Also, these days, nearly all people brush their teeth, wash, and grow up. Toiletries and boxer briefs are commonplace around the globe. The only thing I've really noticed not being available is tampons (the rest of the world uses pads?), which hasn't hindered me all that much. There is no need to pay extra baggage fees for overweight sacks of shampoo and Shakespeare, no need to lug all that around. Why do I constantly feel the need to carry three months' worth of soap when I know it's available wherever?

On the other side of my family, a subtler thing had happened: My stepfather, a former Eagle Scout, continuing REI enthusiast, and lifelong Apple user, instilled in me a love of gadgetry. Even down to a cool new spring-loaded carabiner—simple things like that—a quirky new twist makes me pause for just a minute to ponder whether or not I need something, as demonstrated with my fine collection of portable electronic devices.

It's not completely my fault. Every time I visit my parents in California, generously, I'm given the latest innovations in from the iFamily. Currently, my wife and I (we each receive iStuff) travel with one iPod Shuffle, two iPod Classics, one iPod Touch, an iPad, and my laptop with its accompanying three external hard drives for films, music, and data back-up, respectively. We live abroad, on the move, so there is no choice but to carry them with us, wires, chargers, and all. I remember having the same living room TV throughout my entire childhood.

Ironically, I (most of us, I think) travel and live abroad to somewhat escape these trappings, to take life full-on rather than filtered through web browsers. We keep in touch, but by and large, we are trying to get out from in front of the computer screen, the television, off of the couch, away from work, into the great wide adventure of old. Then, with my collective of mobile electronics, I manage to bring iChat, Words with Friends, and *How I Met Your Mother* everywhere.

Lesson #3: The Worldwide Web

God, it's so convenient. I stream college football, read the daily Yahoo! News fluff, and get on a roll with a TV series, download the six existing seasons, and spend days incapacitated. It's a little easier to justify because this is my life, not just a six-week tour, but sometimes it seems like I could be anywhere. In a bad way: I could do this in Memphis just the same. What's more, 90 percent of the time I'm not even using the Internet to access something defensible, just watching a little YouTube or keeping up with the playoffs.

Unfortunately (fortunately—I don't know), Wi-Fi is truly worldwide. Even in the mountain jungles of Guatemala, people are ignoring the valley view and bubbling volcanoes beyond to check the latest Facebook status, leaning over to ask if the Internet is working when pages open too slowly. I love it. I hate it. I think one portable Wi-Fi-ready device is enough for any traveler, and once a day is responsible use. Now, if I could just follow my own advice.

I would be remiss not to include my mother in this kaleidoscope of blame, so I must say that what she did to me was more subtle, not exactly sneaky or malicious, but rather something her mother also did to her, and probably mother's mother and so on as you go through the lineage. In me, she instilled the compulsion to collect things, to take that which I like and buy 40 or 50 similar versions of that thing, whatever it may be.

I remember ceramic clowns on the bookshelves, cases, and surfaces of our house. There was, in my own room, a collection of baseball pennants so large that it had made it all the way around the top of the wall and had begun to creep down. Hundreds of a particular type of pottery, ceremonial masks in the bathrooms and stairwell and corners of everything, and at least 15 different options, napkin rings and all, of table settings—why only have one of what you love?

She was the first person ever to take me out of the country, the first ever to show me the wonders of flexible price bargaining in dusty tourist markets, and it was on our trips to Tijuana, an hour drive from her home, that I developed my own insatiable drive to collect. It started with blankets, pot pipes, novelty T-shirts, and chess sets—the souvenir classics—and has only mutated into more hippy-ish versions of them, i.e. sarongs, hookahs, tie-waist pants, and juggling balls.

Lesson #4: Souvenirs

I know they are meant to be irresistible: All of us wandering around Southeast Asia in Vietnamese fisherman's pants, chicken-bussing through Guatemala with our Mayan textile shoulder bags, or whipping out the Turkish tavla (backgammon) set to have a game whilst puffing the hubbly-bubbly and sipping tiny cups of coffee. We need all these things to blend in culturally—ahem—in the hostel communal area and the expat bar.

My mistake has always been that I just completely join the revolution. I negotiate for a better price by buying ten of the same thing, as I did with those damned fisherman's pants, with the Mexican blankets, with different Chinese board games I've not learned to play. Then, the next place I go to, I find ways to enlarge the collection back home—things in a box in my dad's guest room closet. In other words, my unfollowed advice stands as follows: one of whatever is probably enough to remember somewhere.

Ultimately, I suppose, regardless of whatever influences we've had upon us, we are left with only ourselves to blame. My parents were never backpackers, never international travelers, or remotely unkempt in any way. I don't remember them ever having a luggage talk with me, nor are any of them excessive users of Facebook, readers of ESPN, or experts at mahjong. Thus, some of the packing miscues of the past have to fall on me as the responsible party.

Bags, in particular, are a problem. In the past few years, I've come to accept that, within me, there is a certain unhealthy obsession with bags. I buy one in nearly every country, often packing the previous country's away into the new one so that I don't have to contend with one more strap on my shoulder. Then, an assortment of bags is left hanging on the back of a door somewhere, waiting for when I do such-and-such activity for which this one would be perfect.

The coup de grâce, however, is my backpack, which, in the past five years of travel, has been changed four times. My wife is still using the same one she took packing through Europe before we met. She lives with broken zippers and dirty material, reoccurring mold growth due to a bad shampoo spill in early 2007. I now have a massive wheeled duffel-backpack so that I don't have to carry mine through airports. If only the carrying were my only problem.

Lesson #5: It's All in the Bag

The troubles with my current bag are as follows: 1.) I don't have to carry it most of the time, so a certain beast-of-burden limitation normally present for backpackers doesn't exist for me. 2.) I can fit far, far beyond what I need in it, leading to temptation, such as bringing more books, juggling balls, devil sticks, and economy-sized bottles of Dr. Bronner's Peppermint Soap. 3.) The combination of not carrying it and being able to pack more equates to costly results.

In 2011, Emma and I moved to Moscow. In the terminal check-in, we discovered that not only were there weight limitations on checked baggage but on carry-on, as well. So, the normal reshuffling and overstuffing of heavy items from check-in to carry-on—it couldn't happen. I left about half a garbage can of stuff, including some shoulder bags from around the world, in the Heathrow terminal, and still paid $175 in baggage fees.

It seems, despite all the self-inflicted lessons, I've still not learned that being able to fit everything in a bag doesn't necessarily mean I've not over-packed.

View Photos in This Set

The Bibimbap Man

When the last of the meal carts comes rumbling down the aisle, I shun the safety of spaghetti and opt for bibimbap, whatever that is. *Spaghetti is behind me now. Bibimbap is where I am these days.* I position my tray table and never question my talent for eating with chopsticks. Forks are a thing of the past, too. Lots of things are.

Boarding the plane this morning, there was every confidence of change to come, and the plan is working. I've not taken advantage of the free alcohol offered on international flights. I have not smoked a cigarette or a joint or slept with someone's wife. I have not used a cell phone or checked my email. I have not looked at Internet porn. No neglected birthdays, denied invitations, forgotten Mother's Day presents. My life is righting itself. I've not even made it to Korea yet.

Some people sort out the mishaps of life with marriages, divorces, shopping, eating, talking, psychiatry, mind-altering substances, and whatever else there is. I chose to move to Korea when "sorting out" was no longer as appealing as starting anew. I wanted to cut the people at my farewell gatherings out of my immediate existence. I could no longer fool them with myths of rehabilitation. They'd seen me drift for too long and too far astray.

Even so, my old friends support the new me because good friends do that sort of thing. They would have no idea what bibimbap is, but if they knew I was eating it, they'd be excited for me. They don't fully understand why someone would want to go to Korea, but by and large, they are encouraging my going. I've simply explained the whole ordeal as a bout of self-exploration and yearning for worldliness, but really, I want a new me with new friends who have no idea I'm crap, in a new place where people can't speak enough English to question me, making new memories.

People have told me how much I'll learn, how great this will be for me. We've talked about food and culture and producing half-Asian babies. In reality, I've signed a year contract to teach children English, knowing a fair amount about the subject but having no idea how to change a diaper or wipe someone else's ass. Being around kids makes me nervous, year contracts even more so, but the whole idea is that things will be different. I will be different. That's the experiment: can one run far enough to escape himself?

When the bibimbap arrives, the prepubescent kid sitting next to me offers up lessons for how to eat it. He's Korean. He tells me he's been studying in the U.S., away from his family, for almost a year, and he tells me to put the packet of red sauce that looks like ketchup on my bibimbap. "It's gochujang," he says. "It's spicy. We put it on everything." I take his advice. Using one of my chopsticks, I stir the mixture of rice, lettuce, pickled vegetables, and fried egg. It looks a mess, a grotesque mix of textures and colors, but tastes better. I eat it all so as to be polite.

My empty bibimbap dish departs in the hands of a flight attendant wearing a Disney-store-blue skirtsuit with a sort of architectural hat. She's Korean, which excites me in a creepy way. The bilingual arrival instructions create a warm feeling in my stomach that turns over the new cuisine filling it. I watch the computer image of our plane until the landing gear drops with a mechanical thud. The 14-hour flight gave ample time to think this through. Korea is no longer just a party conversation of well-wishes. The time for talk is over.

My flight arrives at around 9:30 at night, and Mr. Kim, tall and lean, helps me with my luggage, the ATM, and buying a bottle of water for the "maybe two-hour" ride from the airport to wherever he's taking me. Mr. Kim tells me he's the one who'd written the emails—shattered English with surprising punctuation—and I fake being impressed before remembering the new me doesn't *fake*. The new me will be caring, concerned, honest, and thoughtful from the inside out, and I now feel sincere regret for mocking Mr. Kim in my head. *We* were only being pleasant.

Before we leave the parking lot, I have a quick phone conversation with a man named Mr. Jeong, Mr. Kim's and my boss, in which he formally welcomes me to Korea and checks that all is well. It is a failure, with Mr. Jeong chopping our language to bits and me supplying only affirmative and negative grunts, unwilling to make the polite conversation enjoyable for him. The old me was fine with being awkward; the new me loves interchange with strangers because that's how you get to know new people. Mr. Kim asks if I like the radio, and I say yes as he cranks up the volume. He's missed the point, but I don't fault him for it.

Stuck in traffic, Mr. Kim asks me about LSU, or more so, tells me about Florida. We talk about SEC football, and I find out that he went to college in Gainesville when he lived Stateside. He liked to drink beer with the Gator fans and is one himself. By default, by ranking, LSU fans don't often like Florida fans, but I don't care about football that way anymore. I don't care about Tim Tebow's jump pass from the goal line during his freshman season or his smarmy Christian ideals. For the sake of conversation, I ask if any games are televised in Korea. They aren't, which now seems annoying.

A pop song twinkles on the radio, and Mr. Kim adjusts the volume again because he believes the song is good. I can't believe that someone could look at me—thick beard, faded clothes, long hair, help me load my guitar into a van—and think a five-piece harmony of boys would appeal to me. I squint at the lights of the seventh tollbooth we've gone through. The new me is going to be tolerant of certain musical tastes that make no sense. From now on, bad taste is okay. Dancing is still out of the question.

I cannot help but notice that my landing in Korea has not created one of these afternoon-at-the-coffee-shop, sports-are-for-Neanderthals, conversational people with 'NSync in his CD wallet ("For the ladies, you know"). New hopes are trailing through my head like smoke from spent fireworks. I haven't changed just yet, but there is still the plan of the new me. I'm looking for a compromise.

Nathan, one of my new bosses, lives in an apartment with three other colleagues. Before, I just worked with people, but now they're colleagues, carrying a level of sophistication that surpasses my former restaurant coworkers. Mr. Kim takes his shoes off at the door. The old me probably would have just worn mine in the house and waited for someone to declare a "no shoes" rule, but I am learning to follow Mr. Kim's lead. He's a good man, an SEC fan in Korea. The jet lag is sinking in.

A tall blonde, Grace, offers me some of the dinner she's cooked: spaghetti. I decline and neglect to tell her that the days of spaghetti are behind me. I am a bibimbap man now. Nathan—blond, too, and a woman—gives me a firm handshake. The old me assumed Nathan was a man. The smallest blonde, Hannah, who answered the door, hands me a beer, which I accept because it's polite and not because that's my general reaction to booze. Three blondes offering a buffet of handshakes, dinner, and drinks seems an unlikely introduction to working in Korea. They look nothing like the flight attendant.

I throttle down my beer while answering "yes" or "no" to some getting-to-know-you questions. Mr. Kim makes several phone calls. In Memphis and in Baton Rouge, I lived alone, but in Korea, that's not me. I'll soon be sharing an apartment. The old me would be groaning about having to live with people—probably to his new roommates—but the new me just wants some rest. We say goodbye to the blondes, who sadly are not the roommates, and Mr. Kim and I get into the elevator, waving as the doors slide closed.

He presses 10, then places the palms of his hands on his hips before looking up at the ceiling, then at me. I've never lived above the second floor. I've never lived in a building with more than four floors, which are a lot of floors for where I'm from. I think about climbing all those flights of stairs every day. You don't just stop hating elevators, no matter where you are or who you become. What if I forget something only to realize at the bottom? This could be exhausting. My eyes grow heavier with each floor we pass.

Two more blondes, a man and a woman, are waiting mid-living room. They introduce themselves as Canadians, but lack the cliché "eh" after questions—*How you doin', eh?*—and "about" doesn't sound like "a boot." They are my new roommates, strangers, but normal people live with strangers all the time, right? Sitcoms are made about unlikely roommates where all parties really grow in their appreciation of different people's over-the-edge oddities: *Oh no, Billy and his date are naked on my laundry again—ha, ha.* They both stare at me. Neither offers me a beer or spaghetti.

We've barely exchanged names, but Mr. Kim announces it's time to go. We've not yet even gotten uncomfortable with standing in front of each other. I'm going to a motel because the roommate that I'm replacing hasn't moved his crap out of my room yet. The only me wishes for a question or two more before this new collection of *friends* abandons me in the middle of Where-the-Hell-Am-I, Korea. But my roomies-to-be offer farewells, and Mr. Kim and I get into the elevator, waving as the doors slide closed.

The Rex Motel has a red neon sign that stretches vertically, the writing in English and moving from top to bottom. We park in a dark alleyway where Mr. Kim and I negotiate who's going to carry what of my luggage up to the room. The elevator, the lobby, and the room all have soft neon lighting and no music. We take our shoes off before stepping in to stack my cases. Mr. Kim shows me the television and the bathroom and how to put the key in this little box near the door to make the electricity work.

"Everything okay?" he asks.

"Yes."

He gives me a card with the hotel name and address on it and a card with his name and numbers on it. He puts his shoes on, and I follow his lead. He's going to leave me here. We walk back downstairs to the van, where he lights a cigarette for the new me, who has decided smoking might not be so bad in these situations. He says he'll call to check on me tomorrow, and I immediately look forward to it. He waits until my cigarette burns down to the filter.

After Mr. Kim drives away, the elevator climbs up to the third—no, fourth—no, third floor. Flashing my key and a smirk to the lone receptionist, I make my way down the silent, soft-neon-lit corridor to my room. Inside, a motion-sensor light comes on to illuminate the foyer, about three feet squared and sunken, and after an accidental step into the bedroom, I leave my shoes behind. I jingle the keychain into its little box and watch the room change from dark to dim. The sleepiness wears off now that no one's around.

Lying on the bed, a huge motorized lump wheels in slow circles and makes it necessary to move always to the right of or left of the mattress. There is a condom, an ashtray, and a box of tissue on the bedside table, a photo of a naked Korean woman anticipating ecstasy on the wall, her phone number printed beneath the picture. A small table holds a couple of instant coffee packets and two cups, and I know there is an energy drink but no tiny bottles of booze in the mini-refrigerator from when I checked earlier. The pieces come together. This is a special place I'm staying in.

Moans soak through from the adjacent room. I try to read, to ignore the TV, because the old me read too little and watched too much. The sole window in the room opens above the headboard and offers a view of construction materials in a little square spot in the middle of the building. Through it, I can look up and see the stars. Reverting back to thoughts of my old home or old town or old friends or old habits, the new me decides it's okay to watch TV in these situations.

I discover two English-language shows on television. Both are movies; one is Playboy. The old me used to become enthused when hotels would have Cinemax because of the "skinemax" programming that comes on after 11, but here at the Rex Motel, I watch *Godzilla* instead of Playboy. *Godzilla* does not improve in Korea in a love motel that typically rents by the hour, on a bed with a motorized help-you-cum device, and the arm's reach availability of tissue and a condom, if say a quivering leather-bound Asian beauty mistakens into the room. This is what I've run to for cleansing.

The old me would have sat in a stupor with a movie about a pre-historic dragon of destruction running loose in New York. He would have been content to mock the filmmakers and doubt the integrity of the actors who would sign on for such drivel. *Who in the hell writes this shit?* he would say repeatedly in a room that only he occupied, and he'd watch it to the very end. At which time, a prompt flip through the channels for softcore girl-on-girl action would commence. The new me is above all this stupored mockery but not the misogyny. Godzilla has barely made it to New York, and I'm spent.

The big hoax of the Playboy Channel is that, once that crumpled wad of Kleenex hits the floor beside the bed, there's little left in the way of entertainment. You might as well put on another Hollywood block-buster 1950s dragon-based remake until your fluids replenish. You yearn for a Gatorade. The whole process is why I'm in Korea in the first place: I put all my energy into something, become bored, and change the channel. Now, my options have spiraled into Matthew Broderick or a bubbly blonde bouncing on top of a skinny guy. Has anything improved?

I look at the traveling trunk my father bought me, my guitar case, the backpack I bought three years ago for a trip to Costa Rica with an ex-girlfriend, and the stained pits of the T-shirt I'm wearing to bed. I look at these things transposed against the fake gray wood-grain paneling, the motion-sensor light that shuts on and off the television, the collection of cover-the-smell potions on the vanity, and I know you never start anew. You only pile your crap in a new room and hope there's enough closet space to hide it all.

I mock *Godzilla* because there's nothing else to do. When that grows dull, I mock the bubbly blonde because she probably really does believe in her acting. And Mr. Kim, the spaghetti dinner, the Canadians, even though they didn't actually say "eh" or "a-boot." I mock the Korean educators who have flown me over to teach their youth. The new me sighs, while the old me lights a cigarette, slips the complimentary condom in his backpack, and makes use of his new ashtray.

Why did I turn the TV on? Why can't I turn it off? Ultimately, I switch to Asian ESPN, returning to my roots of all sports all of the time, and ignore the co-ed couple's golf program. The new me attempts to sort through the old me, who only keeps the television on to have some soft light and company. The walls of the room lean in to watch this unfolding of self. The new me decides that one day isn't enough to declare this thing a failure, and in the end, I know it's going to take more than location to make me a better person.

The old me chants, "I told you so. Thousands of miles and nothing is different."

In the year following, the new me became a vegetarian (bibimbap is a vegetarian dish of rice, vegetables, a fried egg, and spicy pepper sauce); began a career in EFL teaching (eight years to date), including over two years of volunteer work; and met my wife-to-be, Emma, a fellow teacher, British not Korean—all of which led me to living in nearly 10 different countries, traveling to nearly 40, developing friendships with people on every continent except Antarctica (though my wife does know a pilot who served there), and going. The old me has come to accept that the bibimbap man abides.

View Photos in This Set

The Other Side of Texas

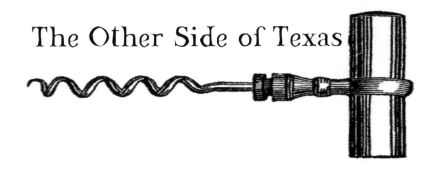

> "Writers facing the problem of Texas find themselves floundering in generalities, and I am not an exception. Texas is a state of mind. Texas is an obsession in every sense of the word."
>
> —John Steinbeck,
> *Travels with Charley: In Search of America*

John Steinbeck married into Texas and "studied the Texas problem from many angles and for many years." I, too, have always found the country-state troublesome, a place I've inevitably ended up, pulled in by forces not under my control. Like Steinbeck, I've married into the hype, or at least my father did, which pulls me in just the same. Where it comes from escapes sound explanation, but within me, there is a seed of bitterness that seems to grow and flower by the year, a fruit something akin to a prickly pear that just oozes Texas.

Being from Louisiana, I could attribute it to a Napoleonic complex, jealousy over, as a child, having to drive to Houston to ride a rollercoaster or to watch a big-league game. I grew up borrowing Texas for its baseball and its amusement parks. The tides twisted when Astroworld and Waterworld were razed some years back, and Baton Rouge suddenly sparkled with lesser-known developments like Blue Bayou Waterpark. Unfortunately, no Texan would ever go east for aquatic-themed fun. They'd just build a new park of their own if that's what they wanted.

As an adult and expat, on more occasions than not, I have to explain that I'm from the state next to Texas. First, I cite Hurricane Katrina, jazz, or Mardi Gras, hoping for some understanding of general location for "Where in the U.S.?" but ultimately, it's always Texas that solidifies my roots. It's not something that particularly pleases me, and from my experience, most proud Texans wouldn't particularly want a foreigner (as in: not from Texas) representing the state. Nonetheless, until *Swamp People* goes international, we—Texas and I—are both stuck with it.

If that isn't bad enough, my father moved to Katy, outside of

Houston, about 12 years ago to work out his remaining years at Exxon-Mobil's headquarters. Then, he retired there. Then, he married a Texan, and together, they moved up to rural northeast Texas where she was raised, where the feeling of being surrounded permeates from the soil, the oil pumps spreading throughout fields, nodding nonchalantly as you drive by. Now, when I visit the U.S., A.K.A. Dad's house, it's in Texas that I find myself, regardless of where my heart may lie.

> "I thought I knew Texas pretty well, but I had no notion of its size until I campaigned it."
> —Ann Richards,
> 45th Governor of Texas (1991-1995)

This year, my wife's father flew from England; my wife and I migrated north from our home in Guatemala; and we all congregated in the tiny town of Kerens (pronounced Kurns) where my dad and stepmother have erected their Texas-sized retirement home, some 20 miles outside of Corsicana, Texas, a couple of hours south of Dallas, and three or so hours north of Houston. It is now Kerens where I go to visit "home," so as a budding world vagabond, I figured it would behoove me to view it as a traveler might, to take in the sites and to grow in my appreciation.

Thus, it was on the ride from DFW airport that the tour began. My new stepmother, Melanie, who has a historian's knowledge of all things Texas, began by pointing out the lights of a factory run on coal. The lights, all that we could see in the pitch black of night, crawled up along a conveyor belt that took coal from the ground to the top of the furnace. The rest of the ride was backroads, dark, with only the occasional spot where deer had been seen, a herd of buffalo is being raised, and ultimately Richland Chambers Lake comes into view, near which my father has settled.

Richland Chambers Lake is manmade, the result of damming up two creeks, the Richland and the Chambers, to fill the valleys betwixt them, creating the third-largest inland lake in Texas, a state obsessed with the size of things. The 45,000-acre body of water is promoted as an angler's paradise, but the reservoir's primary function is to act as a water supply for Ft. Worth. Mostly, though, a series of small communities, largely retired, have sprouted up around it. It isn't the type of place people not already in the immediate vicinity would visit, not to say it isn't lovely.

Turning into my father's housing estate, which consists of two lakeside developments, oil wells take root every half-mile or so along the road, a mix of broken asphalt and gravel that splits massive plots of land. The fields are alternated to raise cotton and soybeans, a hobby for the owner who has long since made his fortune on what is beneath the ground rather than above it. When we finally turn onto my father's street, his house is beneath the lone streetlamp for literally miles, one he paid to put in himself.

It's a funny thing visiting places. I've been to Bangkok, Cairo, and Berlin and consider myself as having experienced the countries they are in. I've lived in Moscow and Istanbul and, despite spending very little time out of those cities, feel immensely in tune with the cultures of Russia and Turkey. For nearly every year of my prepubescent life, I visited Houston, comfortable that Texas could be summed up by the Texas Cyclone, Fiesta supermarkets, and the Residence Inn where my father liked to stay. This Texas was definitely different. It was hilly, eerily quiet.

> "If I owned both Hell and Texas, I'd live in Hell and rent out Texas."
>
> —Mark Twain,
> reiterated by Philip Henry Sheridan,
> or William Sherman

Kerens, a city of fewer than 2,000 people, has one claim to fame: the birthplace of Big Tex, a massive statue of a cowboy used as a symbol for the Texas State Fair. Big Tex was originally built in 1949 to be the world's largest Santa Claus statue and was converted after a couple years. Other than that, the town has a Mexican restaurant that gives cans of beer away because it can't get licensed to sell liquor, and an unexpected secondhand store, the Thrifty Cowboy. It takes us a good 10 minutes to get there. It was nearly half an hour to anywhere else.

So, what I was given was a picture of leisure living in rural Texas. In the mornings, deer eat corn my father or stepmother pile in little mounds around the yard every evening. Neighbors drive by on golf carts (there is no golf course, but everyone has a cart) throughout the day, sometimes stopping for a quick chat from the confines of their vehicle and the rest of the time delivering friendly waves. In the evenings, the deer come back. Once, my father hooked a trailer to his farm tractor, set up some camping chairs, and drove us around the neighborhood.

Our days filled with trips into Corsicana, some 20 miles away. En route, we'd look for buffalo in the buffalo field and note the Russell Stover chocolate factory. Reaching the edge of the city, I always admired an old red train depot. We dined at local joints, a Mexican restaurant with $1.50 margaritas and special mustard-y salsa, as well as a place called the Cotton Patch, where the first four lunch specials were different chicken-fried meats, including chicken. We visited craft shops, dollar stores, and admired the synagogue across from the HEB supermarket.

On the surface, it was a decent destination: wildlife, bargain shopping, unique local cuisine, cheap booze, a large body of water, and notable architecture. There was quirky history to appreciate and an undeniably specific culture with its own traditional dress, methods of transportation, and strong national (state) pride. We were being exposed to it all, and on Daddy's coin to further sweeten the tea. We were at a homestay of sorts on a homestead of sorts, and our local hosts were tending to our every need and whim, eager to show us the best of what east-central Texas has to offer.

> "Since you have chosen to elect a man with timber toe to succeed me, you may all go to hell, and I will go to Texas."
>
> —Davy Crockett

We arrived in Texas on Election Day, and to the dismay of many there, Barack Obama had won his second term with unexpected ease. Now, over 100,000 Texans have signed a petition to secede from the United States, a reoccurring vendetta for independence-minded Texans. One upcoming gubernatorial candidate, Larry Kilgore, has even gone so far as to change his middle name from Scott to SECEDE. To be fair, many cities—Austin, El Paso, Houston, included—signed petitions to secede from Texas and to remain in the U.S. As well, all 50 states eventually drafted their own petition, with Louisiana garnering over 25,000 signatures.

Regardless, and though opinions obviously vary, I've always found a certain fog of conceit to hang around the Lone Star, a need to celebrate all things Texas, cling pridefully to the death penalty, household armories, and the like. Texas is the only state flag flown an equal height to the national flag because it once was a country. After enjoying nine years as its own nation, the 28th state, annexed into the U.S. in 1845, has simply never fully embraced equality with its 49 neighbors and constantly seems to flex and flaunt its economic muscle and geographic size. My stepmother told me that, as if to impress me with Texas' status.

Visiting rural Texas puts one into the thick of it. Big trucks dominate the roadways and guns fill as much of the conversation as they do closets. Ironically, on the day Texas reached 80,000 signatures, we visited a new local attraction, the Pearce Civil War Museum at Navarro College and its accompanying Western Art, i.e. cowboys and such, Museum. On the tour, our guide noted how Robert E. Lee's photo was above Ulysses S. Grant's, explaining that they had originally been the opposite, but enough patrons complained that they changed the display.

There was also one painting that Mr. Pearce had spent over a million and a half on, the most ever spent on "Western art." How Texas can one get?

A few days later, we went to the Texas Ranger Hall of Fame and Museum in Waco. The city made headlines in 1993 when religious leader David Koresh and the Branch Davidians had a 51-day standoff with the FBI before setting the "Ranch Apocalypse" alight while inside, but it has long housed the Ranger Hall of Fame, as well as the Dr. Pepper Museum, which we missed due to time constraints. The Ranger museum shows an impressive collection of guns, including a couple used to ambush Bonnie and Clyde. The highlight, however, was the Hollywood room, with the full outfit of the Lone Ranger and a Chuck Norris, A.K.A. "Walker, Texas Ranger," display.

All this is to say that Texas, like any country, has its quirks and characters, things we like and don't like, agree and don't agree with, but without a doubt, it's unapologetically itself. Citizens oblige you in the history and are unabashedly proud of being Texans, so much so that the state has its own unique blend of culture shock. The peculiarity of these attractions brings to mind touring a cigar factory in Havana and visiting the Seoul Museum of Chicken Art: they are inimitably of the place and could exist nowhere else honestly.

> "Some folks look at me and see a certain swagger, which in Texas is called 'walking.'"
> — George W. Bush,
> former U.S. President, Texas Governor,
> and Quote Master

It's inevitable that I take Texas for granted. It's been there all of my life, like a richer, bigger, more handsome older brother (which I also have). Louisiana is the birthplace of jazz, the land of Cajun cuisine, and the home of Mardi Gras, but it's only in certain knowledgeable circles—chefs, musicians, flashers—that the state gets any respect. Thus, I've had to learn to appreciate the history but to find life beyond our borders. Maybe I've earned the right to grill the dopey giant that is Texas: I've moved off into the world, but Texas has remained firmly rooted where it has always been.

Then, sitting at the Cotton Patch restaurant in Corsicana, Texas, a man walks in donning a 10-gallon hat, his pants tight beneath a belt buckle tilted askew by belly overhang, his shirt starched and tucked, all accentuated by a bushy mustache. Emma, a lifelong John Wayne fan, stopped reading the menu to lean over and ask me: "Is that real?" From the other side of her mouth, she made sure her dad saw the authenticity.

It suddenly seemed so obvious. I got the same feeling in Moscow when I realized people really did wear big furry hats. *It's just like the movies.*

From abroad, we the people of the United States often get heaped into one scoop of vanilla ice cream, melting atop our apple pie world, so it's easy to forget how diverse and exceptional each place can be. Would Emma and her father have seen that cowboy (more likely dressed for show than for saddle) had my father retired in South Florida or Cape Cod? Would they have seen the monster trucks, oil rigs, or longhorn cattle in New York or Chicago? Would they have seen the golf cart brigade, taxidermy armadillos, or Texas-sized houses amongst those expansive yards?

I won't say it's now a favorite destination of mine, nor will I insinuate that its attractions are superbly suited to my interests. For me, Texas will always be Texas, even with a newfound appreciation for the little lean-to towns between boxed-brownie developments and a pursed-lip respect for those caricatures who populate them. Having gone in the guise of being a tourist, I can only say that there is another side to things that I had not considered. There is no mistaking that which is distinctly of Texas and not the U.S., and when in Kerens, there is also no escaping it. And that, not El Paso, is the other side of Texas of which I'm speaking.

View Photos in This Set

10½ Lessons in Misadventure Travel

My father brings it up at least twice every time I see him, offering his best version of vicarious travel advice: *Be careful. Uncle Butch got his ass kicked in Tijuana.* Uncle Butch, who looks as his name indicates—six-foot-one-inches of chest and arms with a dimpled chin—was drunk, out of money, and following a stranger to a "nearby" ATM. Though not exactly well-traveled, my father knows this one might not have been Mexico's fault, but I obligingly acknowledge there is still some truth to what he is warning me about: rarely does a trip come off without hitting (or being hit by), stumbling into, or hiding from trouble. Dad's just worrying about the wrong things:

3 Lessons on Getting from Point A to Point C

1. Visa: Not Just a Credit Card

The first time I tried to go to China, I ended up being turned away at baggage check-in. The ticket agent flipped through my passport, before moving on to Emma's (my future wife), ultimately looking up bewildered.

"Where are your visas?" she asked.

At the time, Emma and I, E.U. and U.S. passport holders, respectively, were novices to the world of applying for visas. Until that point, we'd never been to a place where we couldn't just show up and get a stamp, but in China, and it turns out a few other countries, paperwork is integral.

We struggled to find an alternative route, a way to fix our *insignificant* oversight. The agent, sympathetic to our plight, had little choice but to send us packing, or, more accurately, unpacking. There was no way we were going to see the Great Wall that week. Next, please.

In the end, with tickets at about $550 apiece, a $60 four a.m. shuttle ride to Incheon airport, and an $11 bus ride home, we spent a grand total of about $1,200 not to go to China that year. We weren't beaten up, but I'd bet most Tijuana muggers don't get away with half that much.

2. There Is Only One H in Jonathon

Vietnam was only partially my fault: Though we'd been wise enough to get the proper visa this time, the travel agency (we used professionals after the China incident) had spelled my name incorrectly on the e-ticket: Ms. Jo<u>h</u>nathan Eng<u>l</u>es, not Mr. Jonathon Engels. In some sense, it had been my duty to double-check this.

My ticket, though strikingly similar, didn't match the name on my passport. Unmoved by the likeness and the likelihood that a Korean travel agency butchered the spelling, the Vietnamese check-in lady motioned us to stand aside so that viable passengers could get on with business. Next!

I tend to freak out, mutter incoherently (except for the curse words), as my father taught me, but Emma gets an odd calm in these situations: She called the agency, and they sent us new e-tickets for a flight that evening, free of charge. This time the mistake only cost us 12 hours at the airport. Still, if left to my own devices, it would have been another grand down the squat toilet.

3. How to Get Down in Central America

As most adventurers know, the interesting travel occurs after the flight, and "chicken buses" are the best: crazy cheap, funky, bright-colors, Christmas lights, expressions for Jesus across the windscreen, three-to-a-seat, a standing-room-only center aisle, max capacity of we-can-take-some-more—One can't get closer to a culture. On my second-ever chicken bus trip, from Guate! Guate! (Guatemala City) to Panajachel, about a four-hour journey, our colorful caravan departed from a greasy, garage-laden barrio. As we pulled onto the street, the driver yelled something in Spanish, after which all of the passengers laid on the seats and floor.

Emma and I shrugged, continuing to gaze from the window until the driver stopped and signaled for us to lie down, too. We, the passengers, stayed that way for about 20 minutes, while we, Emma and I, giggled. My head beneath the window, I couldn't see anything, but she had lain with her head toward the aisle, making her the go-to for when we had permission to sit up again.

We later learned we had driven through a neighborhood where the bus would have been jacked had anyone seen its passengers. Chicken buses are notoriously dangerous, not only from the unrestrained taking of curves and the driver half-attentive while chatting on his cell phone, but also, most notably, from the banditos who prey on the drivers.

3 Lessons on When Money Is the Issue

4. When in Doubt, Western Union

I was unable to get money out because the ATM at Incheon airport rejected my card. We flew to Siem Reap anyway, somewhat assuming things would change in Southeast Asia. Surprisingly, the Cambodian ATMs didn't like my card, either, so Emma and I reached an agreement: she'd handle the cash, I'd handle the airfare, and we'd sort out the balance when we got to England.

A week later, her wallet got lifted, and we were left with $300 to get us through three weeks in Thailand, Malaysia, and Singapore. We went into emergency mode: online banking, phone calls, failure. You can cancel a card, but you can't get a new one overseas. We'd saved for months, and though our money was all still there, in essence, it was gone.

At a bar at the side of the street, drinking away our last however many baht and planning our inevitable retreat, we met two middle-aged Cockneys, who called each other Geezer and Nobby, and they listened to our story like concerned fathers, or at least half-drunk Uncle Butches, then bought us a round as they explained how Emma could Western Union herself. Neither of us had ever used it.

Emma's bank confirmed she could do a money transfer in Bangkok, so we delayed our departure from Koh Chang Island for a free day of snorkeling with Nobby and Geezer on their chartered boat. We financed the remainder of our trip via Western Union, and we learned that, in Cockney rhyming slang, "doing a Richard" means doing number two: Richard the Third, turd.

5. Cambio Now Rather Than Later

At the El Salvadoran border crossing, sketchy-looking characters with rolls of American cash paraded around each passing bus. *Cambio*, they said, pointing at the exchange rate on a nearby digital display. We needed to change money, but the bank was closed. This business transaction, with the shifty hustlers, was the sort you're taught to avoid from birth. So, we decided to wait.

Four hours later, in San Salvador, a lady just shrugged her shoulders: No banks opened on Sunday. I took the emergency dollars from my passport holder and bought tickets to La Libertad and, from there, to Playa El Tunco. Retelling our story in broken Spanish, we found a guesthouse that agreed to give us a credit for the day. *Mañana* all would be well.

In the morning, La Libertad's bank didn't exchange quetzals, nor did the local ATM (singular) agree with our cards. We had no choice but to get on a chicken bus back to the capital, pained to part with the $0.31

apiece. We didn't even have enough cash for tickets back to Guatemala. Not knowing San Salvador at all, we departed the bus when we saw a line of about five banks.

At about the fifth bank, a teller finally took pity on us—two grown people in beach attire, nearly in tears because our stupid quetzals were useless—actually came outside, flagged down a taxi, and explained the situation to the driver before sending us on our way ... to what looked a lot like an old parking garage filled with pawnshops.

There was one grubby *cambio* tucked away in the corner, the kind of place you've probably been taught all your life to avoid. We exchanged all our quetzals without a second thought. After all, this pit is where a legitimate bank, unable to do the job, had sent us. Back in the money, we paid the driver handsomely, vowing never to pass those border guys again without exchanging.

6. *The Inconvenience of Online Banking*

It started with Emma's ATM card being declined in a shop in California, 20 dollars' worth of toiletries and beer, what turned out to be a security signaler for the in-tune international banking watchdogs. She called HSBC, which reported that, though she couldn't fix the problem over the phone, all was well: she could reinstate the card by visiting her local branch—in England.

When Emma's mother tried to solve the problem, the bank canceled online access to the account because someone (Mum) had been given the restricted info. We visited a branch in Orange County, California, and after an hour of confused phone calls, the teller was granted permission to reboot the card but not to give her new Internet passwords. That required being in-person at her local branch, where, presumably, one wouldn't need to bank online.

Nonetheless, the card worked again, with the minor problem of not being able to monitor the account balance. So, we went to Guatemala, where some Colombian card cloner wreaked havoc on one bank's ATM outlets in Antigua. This time the international banking watchdogs didn't cut off the card until a good chunk of dough had been taken out of three machines in Colombia, where, unlike California, which we go to annually, we've never been.

This time the bank notified her of the block and, after she reported the theft, said all she needed to do was visit her online account to verify the withdrawals she did not make. However, her online account didn't work, and there are no "The World's Bank" branches in Guatemala. Consequently, for the next 10 months, while we were volunteering as teachers in a local school, I financed any unforeseen expenditures, redeeming myself for the Southeast Asia debacle.

4 Ways to Escape Life-Threatening Events

7. When Animals Attack

I sprang onto her, a pounce that could have easily been mistaken as before-sunrise friskiness if not for: "Something bit the shit out of me!" I ripped my shirt off and flung it to the floor.

Emma didn't even open her eyes. "Are you sure you aren't just dreaming?" she asked.

Then, I flicked on the lights, and she saw the panic on my face as I searched the discarded garment. Inside the folds, I found a two-inch long scorpion looking fairly irritated, tail poised. I paused. I searched, found something and scooped the thing up and tossed it out the door. Then, with further danger averted, a deeper panic hit me: It had gotten me three times in the chest. Did I need the hospital? Did Emma need to suck the poison out? Was I going to die?

At four a.m., there's no one around to tell you what to do, so we did the best we could: online medical advice. Fact one: Scorpions are known for killing babies and old people. Fact two: Only a small percentage of stings require the hospital. Most can be treated like bee stings. Three: I didn't know if I'd been struck by a baby killer or a bee stinger. It was a scorpion! It looked like a scorpion. I'd tossed it out the door, you know, to avoid further injury.

I sat on the sofa not wanting to slip into unconsciousness and never come out. My chest twitched and burned. I couldn't have slept anyway. I was sure parts of me were going numb, as suggested in the worst-case scenario descriptions of scorpion stings. Emma brought me coffee as I tried to sound fearless: I probably wasn't going to die, so there was no need to wake anyone.

Some three hours later, Drew, the owner of the hotel where we were working, lazed in, surprised to find us huddled on the lodge's couch, and delivered the news that we already knew: my scorpion was of the bee-sting variety. Otherwise, I'd be dead like an old person. Emma continued bringing coffee anyway.

8. Folks Back Home Know More Than You

We arrived in Bangkok with money on our mind: This was the end of the Koh Chang Western Union story. Also, it was New Year's Eve on Khoa San Road, so it didn't seem all that odd that military personnel were everywhere. The crowd, though a bit tamer than expected, was still large and festive, and we were back in the baht.

For three days we took in the sights, tasted the spicy-sweet of street-cart Pad Thai, shopped the crap stalls of the open market, until we finally made it back to our email accounts, where we'd last sent well-wishes the morning before we got on the bus to Bangkok, ready to party. After that, several bombs went off in the city.

Both of our inboxes registered in the triple-digits, full of concerned emails, beginning with drop-me-a-line-to-know-you're-all-right requests, into fourth or fifth attempts of Emma's Auntie Kath, my father, my brothers, Emma's mum—everybody panicked. They'd all gotten in touch with one another. No one had heard from us. A Brit and an American had died in the explosions.

We didn't even know anything had happened. Sometimes, travelers just lose sense of what's going on in the world, even if they're right in the middle of the action. My father claims he was a day away from flying to Thailand to find me. There's nothing sketchier than an old man in Thailand, so check in with folks every now and again. Letting them know you're all right may let you know that you might not be.

9. Riots and Tear Gas: Survive on Cinema

May Day, in theory, works as a time in which the laboring side of the world gets a voice. In reality, in Istanbul, it often comes off more like a day of scheduled rioting. Leaving our apartment that morning, we discovered the police had barricaded our neighborhood, a Kurdish ghetto called Tarlabasi, because *we* were the most likely source of civil unrest.

We probed each street and got turned away until, left with no option, caught in the hotbed of social disobedience, we crawled back into the safety of our actual bed to watch movies all day. At some point, a fire-toting mob made it to our street in a fit of harangues and footsteps, the pace quickening as canisters of tear gas whizzed by our apartment. We leaned our heads against the wall beneath the windowsill to avoid any objects that might be thrown into our house.

When things seemed calm, I finally went downstairs to the bathroom. Upon my returning, Emma was rubbing her eyes, streaming with tears. Though racket of distant disorder was still strong enough to seem nearby, she hadn't resisted peeking out, confirming that things, indeed, were awry. The voices were gone, but the air was still full of chemicals.

By early afternoon, we were well into a Coen Brothers movie marathon. The mayhem had officially dissipated. Down the street from the busted bank windows and stir-up of trash, guys were playing *tavla* at the corner café. A little worse for wear, all the world was right again.

10. Sometimes There Is No Choice

If you live in Guatemala, you have a stick-up story. It just happens. Emma and I had survived over a year and a half, a lot of it in *el capital*, without an incident of our own. Then, on Christmas Day, 2010, while guiding a family of three on a short hike in the mountains above Antigua, the four-year-old son with bouncy curls darting from one stick to the next, two gunmen jumped onto the path in front of us, and our story, as did theirs, came to be.

    I was on my belly in the dirt, a man with a bandana covering his face held a gun slightly askew, not pointing at me, not far from it if need be. His partner started at the back of the group, rummaging through pockets and bags, working his way up to me. I had nothing. It wasn't until he'd gotten to my wedding ring, looked at it, and left it on my finger that I felt sure they weren't going to kill us. The little boy, confused, continued screaming: "Why are they doing this?"

    Being held up resonates much more after the guns are gone, the two men disappearing into the thickets from which they'd come, and you're still alive. Back at the hotel, the adults, who'd all held it together for the boy's sake, cracked. In our cabin, Emma sobbed into my chest as I looked out of our opened door, the one we never locked, into the trees, wondering. It could have been a lot worse. Next time, we might not be so lucky.

That's the thing: there's always next time. I still love to travel, and I don't want to quit, even though bad things happen. If one is to be deterred by muggings, bombs, and riots, then the places available to visit become very miniscule very quickly. The beauty of all these stories is that here I sit, having survived them and loving to tell them, whereas I could be talking about the rise and fall of gas prices in small towns in rural Texas. Which is harder to justify?

    At "home," a lot has gone wrong in the last seven years: school shootings, hurricanes, shark attacks, forest fires, tornadoes, the Mississippi overflowing, oil spills in the Gulf, car crashes, economic crises, Detroit, reality TV continuing to grow. ... There's a lot out there to get you. Despite what happened to Uncle Butch in Tijuana or to me abroad, staying home doesn't necessarily keep you any safer. Besides, the stories, like "reality" TV, are a lot less inspired.

10.5 Bring a Friend

It seems to have been quite useful to have Emma around in some of these circumstances, and for her to have me around in others. Perhaps a traveling companion isn't such a bad idea. Besides the company on long bus rides, a person to leave your bag with on that extended trip to the *baño*, the inevitable mooching when you're out of funds, or smooching in the morning, sharing a moment or two of vagabond travel isn't always the worst offense imaginable.

On Motorcycles with Milkshakes

I recall checking for traffic, but maybe not. The next few seconds were spent wobbling over the two busy lanes of the street in front of the scooter rental place, praying nothing would hit me. By the grace of super-charged battery power, I made it all the way across. The gravel beneath the tires popped as I scraped onto the embankment, pretending the off-road trip had been part of the plan. The bike and I headed about 100 feet north before turning around, still shaky but better, and returning to the point of origin.

The rental guy, a big man, 300 or so pounds, smirked. Emma stared at me, doing her best to subdue the doubt. My little blunder at the beginning of the test run had not gone unnoticed, and I had to spend the next couple of minutes recounting the spring of '01 again to demonstrate my expertise. Relaxed and confident, I handed over my money, and the guy took it for some reason. Emma by an equally strange act of loyalty, trust, and stupidity, after having seen my less-than-convincing trial run, was still willing to betray countless oaths to her family that she'd "never get on one of those" and, in fact, get on one with me.

My love of motorcycles began at about the age of eight, arms strapped around my father as we "tooled" the streets of Baton Rouge on his '86 Honda Magna 1100, a bike styled like a Harley but lacking the thudding-thumping engine. Even though Harleys have the attached nostalgia, distinct sound, and all-American approval, my father and uncles drove Hondas. Harleys are maintenance nightmares, but Hondas are worry-free. I've been told this important fact of self-defense for most of my life. When you don't ride a Harley, it always requires an explanation.

Our familial motorcycle club would stop at burger joints, the lot of us filing through the doors, leather-clad and swollen with gritty pride. We ordered our food to go, so we could lean James Dean-like against the seats and gobble double-stack burgers while checking various gauges and liquid levels. At that time, especially on those afternoons, I thought my dad and his brothers were as cool as it comes, and I, by association and birthright, received the same envious, awed gazes from kids riding in backs of family station wagons, parents prodding them to sing camp songs.

When I was 16, my brother would sometimes show up at the end of my high school football practices. Watching us huffing and wheezing through wind sprints, he propped against his '92 Honda Shadow 750, patient, pulling long drags off a cigarette, as if unaware of the "NO SMOKING ON CAMPUS" sign he'd just swept by. Of course, he'd gone to the same school and knew the rule, but what principal is going to tell a biker where to fire up his cigarette?

From the back of his bike, too masculine now to hug on for dear life, I could see the jealousy in teammates' eyes, my brother and I rumbling along the school drive. We'd go for chocolate milkshakes at Rhonda's Café in town. We bought them to-go and strutted to the parking lot. Again, poised against a cruiser and cool by association, I'd pull hard at the thick malt, pretending the straw was just like my brother's Marlboro.

My father rides bikes. Both of my brothers, all of my uncles, and most of my male cousins do. Every gathering at my grandmother's house, someone throttles in on a new, shining hog, the smell of fresh polish erupting around him as he eases the kickstand down with a new steel-studded boot. The owner ceremoniously grants other riders permission to "take it for a spin," and he nods at the comments about torque and pick-up and surprising comfort. The group stands in a circle, stares, and talks seriously over CCs and power, revving the engine to admire the smooth beat of pistons churning.

Sometimes, my bravery at its highest, all of the riders back inside my grandmother's kitchen with coffee or picking at some potato salad, I'd dare to sit on one of the bikes, stand it up—the kickstand still down, ready to catch if necessary—and feel the spirit of it swaying beneath me, my toes tapping nervously at the ground on either side, just knowing any minute I might take off.

Nearly 20 years after that first ride with my father, I went on vacation to Thailand, a world of scooters, even the largest engine being a fraction of the size of those I'd grown up around. Still, signs were everywhere, in bright colors, with catchy phrases in broken English: "Here Scooter Rent." My head spun a spool of excuses that all came around to finding some way to get my ass on the seat of one of these things. "Motorbike Rent Here Cheap" somehow just made perfect sense.

Sure, my trusty *Lonely Planet* guide had urged readers that only confident, experienced riders should hire a bike, as every year Thai highways claim several tourists. Luckily, I told my girlfriend, Emma, who had, by then, re-heard the recounts of Spring '01 "Tour of Tulsa," this man had experience motorcycling, and not just on some electric-powered, flowered, glorified moped, but on a "real" bike. My fear was completely under wraps, and my desire to get on a scooter was the freaking ribbon on top.

After two days in Thailand, when we found out that the waterfall we wanted to see was a good 45-minute drive away, I knew exactly what to do. It was too far to walk. Taxis were too expensive. But there was something else, a second option, a leaner, more cost-efficient, exciting, ocean-breeze-through-knotty-hair way of getting there: Renting a scooter would cut the cost—not just in half, in thirds. How could Emma argue with that?

"Do you want me to?" I probed. "I wasn't going to, but I will. I hate to miss that waterfall. I mean if you want to go, we're better renting. I'm not paying that taxi driver 40 bucks; that's crazy."

From the time I got my first job, somewhere in my bedroom sat a little wooden box that had been passed down from my father to my brothers to me, and inside that wooden box sat a wad of money known as "the motorcycle fund."

During my freshman year at LSU, I lived with my brother, Chris, of cigarette rule-breaking fame. He'd bought a new '96 Honda Shadow 1100 to replace his older, smaller version of the same model. Every time I came home from work or school or wherever—two in the morning or seven in the morning—Chris was polishing or wrist-deep in grease, having taken the baffles out of the tailpipes.

"Listen to this," he'd said, ratcheting the gas to let out a raucous spitfire of noise pollution and oily smoke.

Chris loved his bike and often took spontaneous half-mile rides through our one-street neighborhood, circling the cul-de-sac and really cracking down before coasting back into the driveway, the cigarette still hanging from his mouth. We'd flip through the latest *Penny Saver* or used-car magazine, hoping to find the right deal for me, hoping any time now I'd be taking those same half-mile runs down Mayberry Street. It didn't happen that year, and Chris moved to Oklahoma for work.

Three years later, I graduated, followed my brother to Oklahoma, and got one of the few jobs my English degree could get me: construction. It was ideal. Not only did manual labor supply me with a closet full of tattered clothes—a biker requirement—but also the money, the insane hours of overtime, to beef up the motorcycle fund. It was the closest I'd ever been to realizing the roar of my own Honda.

Then, we found it in a used-car magazine: a brand spanking new-to-me 1987 Honda Shadow 700, which numerically was 400 less than my brother's Shadow 1100 and, thus, the exact bike for a beginner. We set up a time to see it, test-drive it, but I knew: I was a week away from taking my seat at the table.

When Sunday morning came, my brother was drinking coffee in greasy jeans and a muscle shirt, a leather jacket thrown over the dining room chair. And that's when I realized that I hadn't any idea of how to ride a motorcycle myself. I'd only ever secretly sat on them or ridden what they call—affectionately, of course—bitch. My cousins' smooth transitions from boyhood to bikerdom had fooled me into believing my family was inherently able to do this. I'd have to start with where the key went.

Imagine the embarrassment as I hand over the most money I've ever spent on anything, only to watch my brother, cigarette in position, give it the goose and speed away. I had been reduced to driving the truck home, following *him* on *my* bike. What would the boys at the construction site have said? There would be no hesitation lying about this on Monday morning. Nonetheless, that '87 Honda Shadow 700—it's important to relay this information when talking about Hondas: year, make, model-size, in that order—that '87 Honda Shadow 700 was mine.

By probably the third coat of polish, courage and curiosity got the better of me, and Chris took me to the parking lot of an abandoned grocery store. Lessons started with him swerving around in figure eights before he pulled over to pass the bike on. Just holding the bike up made me nervous. It felt so heavy and sure to toss me away like some pissed-off bronco. Chris grazed through a series of simple instructions, but with my face reflected in the tank, my concentration was less than good.

Then, I heard it for the first time: "Let it out easy," he said, referring to the clutch, which looks like a brake on either the right or left handlebar. The whole contraption more-or-less resembled the cables and whistles of a 10-speed to me—but, of course, better. The bike jumped and died. "Let it out easy," he reminded me. Jump, die. Again and again, we went through this process, until finally, clutch easing out, engine humming with gasoline, I rocketed away with no idea of how to turn.

I could make out the wood grain on the boarded-up windows when my hand, perhaps instinctively, though turning the bike hadn't been instinctive, clutched the brake in time to avoid the 10-mph head-on collision with the former Super Fresh Grocery. The bike swayed a little to the left, and my '87 Honda Shadow 700 shifted off-balance. I fought like mad to keep it from flaying, handlebars out and foot pegs kicking, onto the pavement.

Chris is one of those special people who finds real humor during a situation like this, the thick, deep echo of his laughter blasting from across the cracked asphalt. He sauntered up, he with his Marlboro, and we got it back on its tires. "Let it out easy," he reminded me. Jump, die. My brother gripped the back of the seat, the way a father gives bicycle lessons when you're five, and sent me away with these last words of encouragement: "You HAVE TO lean, or this thing will not turn."

Eventually, I rode in figure eights that were doubly larger than my brother's; the tightness of your figure reflects your skills. I drove it home that evening, my ass puckered tight enough to play a trumpet.

I practiced after long days of work, over the next couple of weekends, scratching out a collection of pulverized foot pegs and handlebar ends. I left a fat, deep tire track in the, luckily for me, flattish ditch across from Chris' driveway when turning sharply on take-off still seemed a bit too frightening. Despite whatever mistakes, the pride and ruggedness swirled in me thicker than the maltiest of milkshakes. I was a biker, even if only in my infancy.

When my skills got not-that-bad enough, we took a two-hour trip. Finally, the people in cars, children bouncing in the backs of SUVs, looked at us—at me—with that mix of envy, fear, and confusion that I remembered getting on the back of my father's '86 Honda Magna 1100. They had no idea about the collection of scratches my bike had acquired over the last two weeks, my inability to turn with consistency and comfort, or the unfortunate overflow of gasoline on my tank from when I'd filled up at the start of the trip. To them, I was simply another cool-ass biker out for his Sunday drive.

I learned things on that trip, substantial things. The wind over bridges bullies you on a bike, pushes you hard toward the oncoming lane. Leaning in curves is easier at higher speeds because, if you don't lean, you'll probably die plunging into steeper, less-friendly ditches than those across from my brother's driveway. Gravel doesn't actually do the whole spitting onto a geek thing, but in fact, makes tires slip with bowel-awakening moments of rollercoaster stomach. Bikes remain heavy no matter how far you've driven and without regard for how many people are watching you, and when it dumps over during those idling moments, you have to suck it up, refrain from screaming for your brother, and use everything you've got to lift that machine back upright.

Despite having done another couple of months of riding and having plans to leave Oklahoma for a cross-country trip to see my mother in California, there were still things to be learned. On what turned out to be my last spin on the '87 Honda Shadow 700, I learned that not everyone in cars thinks motorcyclists are cool, and in fact, some drivers don't think of motorcyclists at all.

With only 20 minutes back to the polish and safety of Chris' garage, a car speeding down an on-ramp that merged with the one I was puttering alongside missed me by what seemed like inches—I can't be sure because my eyes closed. I spiked the engine just enough, just in time, to squeeze by—*Oh, my dear God, please no, I'm sorry, Mom*. My body out-rattled my old bike for the remainder of that ride home, and I parked that beautiful '87 Honda Shadow 700 with new leather saddlebags on custom racks, quite content to be leaving it there the next morning when my car would be carrying me across the country.

The whole world of bikerdom had whizzed by with that speeding car. My guts couldn't handle it. The gasoline had completely coursed through my veins. Without even a kindly salute from my fellow bikers, I decided to bow out of the game gracefully with my appendages still intact. I would happily reside in the stories of the spring of '01, riding with my brother. The next morning, I abandoned that low thud-thump that hadn't left my head since I was eight without even bothering to give her a goodbye polish.

But I rode on the ownership for years.

As I examined the bikes on Koh Chang Island, the owner, a Samoan-sized Thai dude with long dreads and a six-inch goatee, came over to help me. He didn't look like some quirky PhD student; he looked like a *bona fide* badass. "You ever ride a bike before?" he asked, just moving through the standard questions, as any responsible businessman would do, as if he couldn't recognize the steeliness in my gaze.

And, somehow, the old visions of the '87 Honda Shadow 700 and that smooth character, those *Easy Rider* hallucinations, were replaced by a quirky, scooty PhD student who also had the shoulder-length hair but in more of an organic-shampoo kind of way. Of course, a Vespa wouldn't exactly be the type of machine my cousins and uncles would queue up to sample. I reassured him, citing vast experience gained in the spring of '01.

Still going through the motions, he suggested a test run, and so I ambled upon the little machine—an automatic, ha! Even less power—and commenced getting through these little formalities. Then, I shot through traffic, wobbled 100 yards down the road, and fought back tears of fear on my way back to the shop. And then, I pretended to be cool with it all. No big deal. Another day on a bike.

After the test run, Emma insisted on my picking her up across the road of peril, which had only just spared my life. She watched as I gassed the thing again, over the road with a battery-powered blast like something out of ground speed tests. Visions of the Super Fresh Grocery flashed before me. It was too late to turn effectively or to brake, but I managed to twist the tire enough to slide into a flowerpot in front of the Koh Chang Washeteria instead of flying straight into the wall. Then, the lighter, easier-to-handle, more energy-efficient scooter dumped over just as readily as an '87 Honda Shadow 700.

Worse, my leg was caught under the right side, my big toe being pulverized like a foot peg. My right hand was buried hard in the gravel and glass beside the building, my left hand struggling to push the bike up enough to slide my leg free. My face was red with heat and terror, and from it, I emitted a helpless wail for Emma's assistance. The massive rental dude had already begun the trot over, his shirt hiked comfortably above the bellybutton of his robust stomach. My brother's hearty laugh pounded in my head. What would the boys at the construction site think of this?

By the time my rescuers had lifted the bike off and plenty of cars had passed, slack-jawed children staring from the back glass with a bewilderment nothing like those received in the days strapped behind my father, it was too late to admit my mistake gracefully. This is what some dreams turn into: a pile of rubble sweating and groaning at the side of the road, a girlfriend already busy reassuring me that there is still some reason to feel cool, two Thai dudes already exchanging snickers as they cart the bike back to the line of other bikes, waiting to be rented by 18-year-old girls on their first vacations away from parents.

Inside the next-door bar, owned by the same guy—he'd graciously refunded my money despite fresh scratches on his scooter—I asked Emma if we could sit and have a drink. I needed time to recover, get the shake out of my hands, and give my toe a moment to mend. I struggled with lighting the last cigarette in my pack, content to have picked up only one of my brother's badass habits, glad that I'd moved past milkshakes and graduated to the dulling effects of an ice-cold beer.

So, early in my traveling career, I got one of the most relevant lessons being abroad can provide: You always learn something about yourself, assess values you might not have otherwise, and get a better grasp of just exactly who it is you are. Best of all, you do it in front of people who'll never see you again.

The Mousehouse

KATHY GILBERT

For Julie, my microbiologist mother

Art Deco Buffalo City Hall, 21st floor
in your white lab coat you peer through an oil
immersion microscope for parasites:
cryptosporidium, schistosomes, filaria, leishmania.

You pause, stand, and gaze out: Lake Erie
iron gray with a winter storm coming,
look toward Black Rock and the lighthouse.

Cynthia, colleague and cohort, a friendly
face in a sea of men, comes in from the Milk
and Water Lab. Her next vacation plan:
a tramp freighter to Egypt on the Nile.

You, who have traveled from the farm in Alberta
to the States; from Depression to Recession;
from daughter, to mother; nowhere else, are envious.

Now a dog's skull to open, a brain to dissect
slicing tissue samples of Negri bodies; prepping
injections for the mice to detect rabies.

You open the door to a closet full of cages.
Mice, hundreds, some with picric yellow painted stripes
indicating they were injected, squeak; the rancid odor,
fetid smell of rodent fur, pours into your nostrils.

Later you will bring one mouse home to me, your
sixteen-year-old daughter, to chloroform, cut,
extract the heart, keeping it beating with a salt solution
on the kitchen table. You want me to be a surgeon.

Scalpel in shaking hand, I realize I don't have
eyesight or steadiness to fulfill that dream; but
with you in mind, I will see rivers of five continents.

Water Sports

NOEL KING

In this dream, a gondolier,
dressed in a Santa Claus costume
is maneuvering his vessel in and out,
over and back, the canal. I suppose
it is Venice. I am his passenger,
am holding your hand. You're in
a head-scarf and Jackie Kennedy glasses.

It segues (the dream) into ski slopes
and we are both making movements
similar to that Santa Claus was;
in, I guess, Switzerland,
are breathless
and kiss at the
end of the
piste.

Finally, there is a
surfboard of immense thickness
and length and we're both astride.
We try to make exact-same
movements to keep on top
but keep falling off
and re-emerging
grabbing our surfboard,
kissing each time we
mount it.
Until this time
and I surface
alone,
splash and panic
panic and splash
and calling out your name …

For the Behaviorists

DAVID L. TICKEL

She called. I gave her
A cheap estimate. I didn't hear from her.

She called
But I didn't know it was her. I

Got into the neighborhood, on the
Street—

I gave her
A realistic, more-expensive estimate because

She'd lost the
First one.

She called. I called her back
All week long—

She'd been at
The hospital, getting—

A skiing accident—more back work. I
Went to work on her house. She

Was hypercritical. I got on
Her cell phone, spoke to her husband
In India.

I
Went back to work, made sure the

New rugs were
In pristine condition.

I'm out one hundred backs
So far.

High & Dry

J. BRADLEY

I stared through the backsides of future loves,
studied the tarot deck of their underwear.
"You're turning into something you are not,"
they might say as the novelty of us
erodes. "I was born to disappoint you,"
I might reply, lower lip hanging, swelled.

"I bet you think it's clever, the new snares,
cock as tether, the promise of forever,"
I said. "Practice makes perfect," I whispered.
The lack of medical insurance quelled
the rebuttal growing hot in my knuckles
against mirrors, keyboards, televisions.

"The best thing you ever had has gone away,"
I want to say and believe it one day.

Two by Night

DAVID S. CROHN

Along the bank of the river was where I meant to dump it. I was driving there, had it in the trunk, wrapped and ready. Then came the lights off the side of the road, a flashing red pair blurry through cascades of rainwater on the windshield. I eased on the gas and saw, standing in front of the open hood of a car, her. A shivering woman, beautiful with tight-lipped worry. I pulled over.

The rain had barely subsided since I'd set out a few hours before, but it was late and the night, dark. I left my headlights on. As I approached, I saw mascara running down her face, and the way the rain had plastered strands of hair across her forehead. The thing in my trunk could wait, I figured.

"Hey, there," I said, both of us stepping into the cone of light streaming from the front of my car.

"Thanks for stopping," she said. She was shifting her weight from one side of her body to the next. On a flimsy silver chain around her neck, a thin crucifix. It reflected the light of my car's headlights in tiny bursts.

"Engine trouble, eh?"

"Yeah, something like that. The, um, transmission?" She was probably right. Through the damp odor of the soaked forest around us, I thought I could smell it, transmission fluid leaking from her car. I stepped in front of the open hood, leaned in, and peered into the engine. No smoke, just some steam from a warm engine in cool weather.

It was then that I hesitated, realized what a bonehead play I'd made. I think she used a crowbar or a tire iron—hard to tell, really. Pain zapped the back of my skull, then, nothing. She smacked me good—hard and true.

When I came-to, the rain had stopped, and she was standing over me—me splayed on the ground and my back propped against the back of my car. *Strong, Christ,* I thought first, to have dragged me from her car to mine. Second, that I knew that crucifix from somewhere that wasn't Sunday School. I was rubbing the back of my head, the first light of day starting to warm the sky.

"Get up," she said, waving my piece and mustering confidence like some gun moll in an old movie.

"Listen," I said, "I don't want any trouble—"

"Shut up," she said. "Just shut up."

"Okay," I think I said. My head really hurt. "You're the boss."

"Get up, and open the trunk."

"Okay." I popped it open to reveal the mess of grimy blankets within.

"Move those," she said.

"Lady, I don't think you want me to do that."

"Just do it." She kept the piece trained on my face.

When I did it, she gasped and started to cry. She covered her mouth with one hand, the gun pointed at me with the other. She kept it together pretty well, all things considered. Seeing your husband like that—dead-gray and wrapped in plastic like tomorrow night's turkey—well, I might get a little rattled, too.

Interstices

KELLY JEAN EGAN

Then a Saturday arrived, whitewashed
in the wake of the evening I first knew

what I knew must be love. I did the dishes,
watched angel hair strands of suds trail from plates

as I swung them from sink to rack to dry.
The kitchen oven's digital clock, surprised

to see me doing fewer than two things at once,
duly froze in its tracks. The present brimmed.

Moments themselves drew close enough to touch
as I dove between the seconds of my tasks.

Somewhere, women were sitting on their knees
in the grass, patiently weaving nets.

There, in my bedroom I folded sunlit laundry,
smoothing wayward creases from pairs of pants.

Is this then all that was ever required?
Love like the piano strokes of an adagio,

each chore a dancer's extended arm arching back.
That afternoon, the sleeves of my freshly dried

shirts were still warm as I returned them,
one at a time, to their drawers.

Because We Were Taught to Love

ANDREI GURUIANU

Mrs. Ivanov and the many rows of the anonymous for company.
So many familiar names.
Carnations on every grave, red flags brushing the ground.

Someone played a toy bugle with murder underneath his breath.
It came out as the happy song of May.
Girls with big blue eyes fidgeted with the folds of their skirts.

Before it even got started the road to glory ended abruptly.
It was full of potholes someone had filled in with dirt and gravel.
Avoiding them made the road seem that much longer.

The Mrs. kept standing in the crowd smiling and singing.
She was by the roadside holding a red carnation and a flag.
It was also red; it wrestled with its own conscience.

Girls Are Cats and Guys Are Dogs

CHRIS BUTLER

Girls are pets.
Guys are wild.

Girls are pussies.
Guys are bastards.

Girls are named after Egyptian queens and cuddly things.
Guys are called whatever four-letter word is hollered.

Girls live in an alley.
Guys reside in the doghouse.

Girls lick themselves clean.
Guys gnaw on their crotches.

Girls purr.
Guys pant.

Girls are fixed from littering kittens.
Guys are neutered to serve their owners.

Girls play with their prey.
Guys chase furry tail.

Girls squat in a box and bury their dirty secrets in the sand.
Guys piss on the perfect tree.

Girls climb atop the perfect tree.
Guys dig up dirty secrets.

Girls hiss.
Guys bark.

Girls are diseased by rabies.
Guys acquire cat scratch fever.

Girls have nine lives.
Guys die seven years at a time.

Girls become the victims of neighborhood sadists.
Guys get hit by a truck.

Barbie Reads of Louis Braille

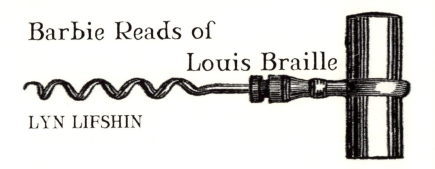

LYN LIFSHIN

how, blinded by
his father's awl
making shoes and
starved to know
and read, he used
what had hurt him
to get to where
he wanted to go,
used the awl
that blinded him,
thinks of him,
tired of just
being a pretty
face, of trying
on clothes, tired
of shopping   she'd
hurl herself through
the glass some
one got her cased
in, fling her
self to the
floor, even if
it meant chipping
a hand or a toe
to show she can
show those who
lust to be so
perfect and thin
that inside she
is empty, can't
bleed, have babies,
age or need a bath
but can, by being
treated as she's

been treated, be broken,
be the loneliest,
not even a belly
button to connect
with what's come
before, or a womb
to have part of
her part of
the future

Homo erectus

KEVIN CATALANO

Henry's wristbones shivered at the collision of aluminum bat to skull, a vibration that rattled his elbows, armpits, ribcage, and belly. He looked around the lightless alley behind the bar before bringing the bat down on the head once more. He was about to run, then crouched beside the man's body and emptied the pockets of the wad of tips. As he was bent, Henry felt stiffness between his legs. He stood, looked down, and there below his belly, tugging at his nylon running pants, a massive erection.

The bar's back door opened, and Henry dropped the bat and ran. Before stepping onto the lit street, he caught his breath, then took out his cell phone and pantomimed conversation as he walked to his car. The dashboard clock blinked 8 p.m. As Henry sped the backstreets, he squeezed his hand down his pants to investigate the erection. *What the fuck?* He punched his leg and bit his tongue, but it was not deterred.

He arrived at the YMCA at 8:07. He walked in bent over to conceal the protrusion from the old ladies working the desk. He grunted and gripped his back as explanation for his posture.

Once out of sight, he hurried down the stairs to the basketball courts, where five guys were warming up.

"There he is."

"Hey, Henry, whaddaya say?"

"Sorry, guys. I was upstairs getting some crunches in. Been here about half an hour."

"Crunches?" The guys leaned on each other, laughing.

"Can we get this game on already?" Kenny snapped, unamused.

"Be right there. Got to use the bathroom first."

Henry rushed through the locker room and into the bathroom stall. He pulled his pants down, and it was still there, throbbing. *Shit!* He proceeded to masturbate, but it was stubborn in his fist, and after a few minutes, he quit. He scrambled to the lockers and began rifling through people's belongings until he found a roll of athletic tape. He wrapped the tape around his wide hips, fastening his erection to his abdomen. He laughed examining the mummified penis. He then pulled his pants up and checked himself in the mirror. It was unnoticeable. Henry exhaled and shuffled out onto the court.

"Let's get this over with," Kenny said. "I want to get to the bar before going home."

"Is Kissy working tonight, Henry?" asked Sanchez, whose name was Paul.

"Yeah, shit, I'll go, too, if Kissy's working," said Walker.

The ball was passed to Henry to inbound. He squeezed it. "Uh, I think she's working. I mean ... I don't know." He passed the ball, then hobbled down the court.

"You *think?* Shit, I'd never let a girl like that out of my sights."

The erection swelled beneath the tape. It felt like a whole loaf of deli meat was strapped between his legs. A basket was scored, and everyone ran back to the other end of the court.

"Why you running funny?" Albert asked.

"Your herpes acting up?" cracked Sanchez, whose name was Paul.

"Too many crunches, I guess."

On the next defensive play, Henry couldn't help but steal a lazy pass at midcourt, and he found himself in a fast break. Henry was forced to sprint as Kenny and he charged toward the basket with only one defender to beat. Henry was given the ball near the goal, and he jumped to score a layup. He came back down the court, his teammates high-fiving him, until Big Dave screeched.

"What the fuck is that!"

Henry's erection had broken free, and it was pointing like a divining rod. The guys moaned and scattered.

"Why you packing heat, Henry?"

"It's the crunches ..." Henry tried. "I mean, the medication I'm taking—it has all these side effects."

Henry fled the gym and stomped up the stairs, barking and smacking at his dick along the way. He Cromagnoned his way out of the Y, hunching and grunting again for the old ladies. Once in his car, he took out his cell phone and called his girlfriend. He got voicemail.

"Kissy, hey, it's like 8:35. I've been at the Y playing basketball for the past hour or so. I'm coming over. I'll be there in two minutes."

Henry sped back through town, bypassing the street that went by the bar. He turned into the apartment complex, jogged down the hall that always smelled of fried bologna and cigarettes. He tamed his erection under the waistband of his boxers, then knocked on her door.

Kissy's eyes were smeared with mascara. She seemed not to recognize him, then collapsed into his arms and wept.

"What's wrong?" he mumbled, clutching her small body, his erection trouncing her ribcage. She suddenly jumped back, looking at his pants.

Kissy was dressed for work, which meant a black miniskirt that barely covered her panties, a low tanktop and push-up bra, big hoop earrings, lipgloss shimmering her pouty, Latin lips. The tingle shot through him.

"Henry, why are you looking at me like that?"

He shut the door and approached her. She kept her eyes fastened on him as she retreated backward.

"I just got a call from the bar," she said, knocking into the coffee table. "Someone murdered Rob."

The erection was leaping forcefully as if trying to free itself from his body. Henry pulled his pants down to his ankles and shuffled forward. She ran into the wall, her eyes wide and chest heaving.

"Henry, I think you should know something," she stammered, reaching under her skirt to roll her panties down her legs. "About me and him."

"There's something you should know, too," Henry said, lifting her off the ground. She wrapped her short legs around his waist as he pinned her to the wall. His hands under her ass, he held her just above his leaping erection.

"About what?" Kissy breathed into his ear.

"About me and him."

White Wolf

CEE

What is my opinion on the subject of
Copyright?
It is the same as my opinion on the subject of
Games that should have been playtested
For four Olympics or so
Before Ever taking money away from one kid's
Parents
Copyright
Is like that,
An iron law of about six words, written with
The Finger of God
With 6,894,620 addenda attached
By humans so angry and harmed
That when they were children and you tried
Trading with them at lunch,
They came back at you like a son of a bitch

Four voices at a high school graduation

VICTOR SCHWARTZMAN

I was trying to listen to speeches
at the high school graduation,
some girl on stage talking wisely
about children becoming adults
but instead what I heard
were two women in front of me,
one blathering without stop.
Women! Hell, I could gossip plenty
Our son got some girl pregnant
She lost it, I didn't hear details
Don't need to hear these two either
so I leaned forward and said be quiet

I was advising my daughter about Mary
when this fool behind us said be quiet
Stop talking about my granddaughter?
about the miscarriage, her future?
the boy who disappeared on her?
Men, I tell my daughter, are trouble
The idiot behind me does not know
Being a parent is important to me
To finish I had to whisper in her ear
Marilyn needed to hear my concerns
A daughter needs her mother for advice
I see her listening to my every word

I was so glad when that man complained
Maybe Mom would finally shut up
but no, she just had to finish, leaning close,
missing my Mary giving her speech
Mom thinks she was so great raising me
What I wanted was to enjoy the moment
Mary graduating, her valedictory speech
to forget, for a time, the mess,
how she fought for what she wanted,
then he dumped her and she lost it
She is so much stronger than I am
I'm proud of the future standing before me

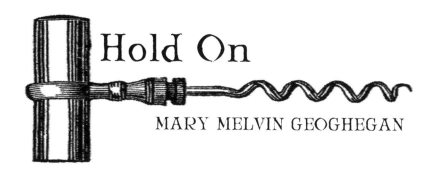

Hold On

MARY MELVIN GEOGHEGAN

as a tooth breaks on an apple.
I can't escape the grief leaving
Streedagh strand in Sligo, and
all those lost from one of the Armada ships,
having managed to swim to shore,
are slaughtered just as they drag
their bodies from the water.

Though I could have swallowed,
or worse broken, another molar.
My tongue can't leave the crater alone,
smooth as the stones beneath my feet
marking a Spanish mass grave.

My Bursting-Up Diploma

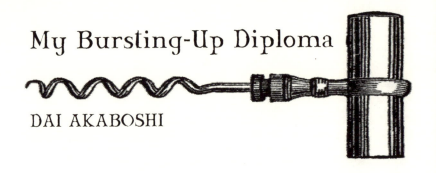

DAI AKABOSHI

Take one more—one more sip before you go, to your worried face.
No need to have one now. I am feeling good, so let me fill up,
have a blessing toast before you go.
Before you wanna quit …

Before you wanna quit, let me tell you about a new girl.
I know you might say, "Another one?" and call her an instant
bitch to ease my life, to get some quick cash, by a little bit of acting
and begging as usual.

She is nice, smart, spontaneous, damaged,
a dive stripper. That's the way I like.
That's her—soon to be ready, another sugar mama
in need of a pet daddy.

You tell me, it's never too late, to hope, better, and dream,
but it gets bitter and sadder.
Once, I did exactly what you told me to.
Nothing great happened. Hell, I don't want a third parent.

All I need is women with ocean-sized sympathies,
endless bottles of hard-ass liquor, dark dream pills,
burning powder, and magical smoke—but a small messy room,
my room, my sad waiting room.

Two men sit in silence. I look smaller.
You take a glass from my skinny arm effortlessly
with your strong hand and throw the glass on the floor.
I know you do but …

To hell with your caring eyes. Tears await to jump off in no time.
In this filthy room, my carpet had a toast for my great loss;
you quit being my pal. I hope no more of this,
but my hands read my mind and reach what it desires.

For one more sip, this is the last one, the last one,
keep telling myself, and I have done that for many years
until I finally lose all my friends. Cheers and Sorry!
I taste a mouthful of hell, and I am ready.
I quit for real, this time—this time.

October

JARED A. CARNIE

And in comes October
Drooling the first winter tragedies
With a wink
And a crooked grin
Of old gravestone teeth.
The heating breaks
And the hot water stops
And our breath taunts us
In the air of our bedroom
And his claws come out.
But still we laugh
Surrounded by candles
And wrapped in blankets
With books and songs
For we recognized
His tattered outfit
Before we met his eyes
And made sure
To make sure
He would have to come
Again.

My Squadron of Choice

BRIAN C. FELDER

I have never been a brigand of hearts feminine,
which may explain my many women friends.
They trust me, I think, because I'm not on their radar;
not a bogey approaching from 12 o'clock high.
It's a good thing overall,
in that they make better comrades than men,
but, still, I am a man
and I enjoy their closeness,
happy to be on their wing tip
where I can see how beautifully they fly.

It Won't Always Be Like This

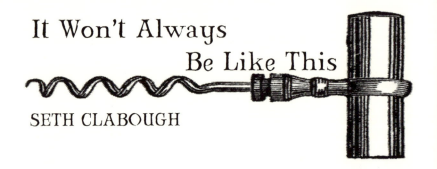

SETH CLABOUGH

At least that's what you'd say when things were bad—before the move to this distant peninsula, before the Havilland Twin Otter flight, before the sky emptied its blue lungs in fatal gusts.

But there's nothing new in loss, or in the way morning in Santa Teresa awakens first in the tops of the old pochotes, breaks free from the tines of playa trees to press its fiery stamp on village & shore.

> I watch it lift into the heart of another day, a day so dry it crumbles underfoot, & it reminds me only of our nights at Villa Serena with laundry lifting on the line, Halloween crabs foraging among dead leaves, the whine of the hammock, the warmth of your bare breasts against my ribs.

You said once the Nicoya Peninsula had such *wet stars*. You called them by name like old lovers. I thought of your freckles as stars, as entire constellations but never said it. I wish I had.

Years have passed and this morning is as far from you as night from day—like it's the other side of it, like it's forever. Our Ruby loved watching the iguanas emerge to mount fallen logs, to bathe in shafts of renegade light.

> She named the red-faced male Gustavo, and the woman who swept our villa said he could open up a leg with the whip of his tail. We shouldn't trust what we feel, Ruby, what we see and hear, how the yigüirro's call squeezes our hearts through its fingers, how the leaves are agitated by the loss of it all.

And I don't mourn either of them anymore. I know they're among the stars that love them, that they press their lips to them, that they burn brighter with their embrace. But I'll still find, on occasion, one of Ruby's toys along the corners of the property and that flick of memory will open up my guts in the sand. And sometimes, when the sodas are closed, after Hector and Angelicia have left with a bag of empty Imperials,

> I'll glimpse my wife disappearing into the fragrant night or find at daybreak, cursive messages from her writ in the swash lines and know she's behind it all, that she's speaking to me, that she's saying, *It won't always be like this*, but I hope that's not true. I know their loss is a presence I can't do without.

Besides, tomorrow the edges of the sky will be bruised purple, & Gustavo will come to sun himself in a little pool of light. Breezes will come & go. We move on or don't, seeking those little spaces we need to survive.

On this remote peninsula, you can evade the threat of moving on. Here, lost voices never grow silent. Here, you can wait for the evening & then see, once more, constellations of wet stars, which were gone & always there.

The Holy Fight

NORMAL

In my almost 70 yrs there has always been a war
In my father's 95 yrs there has always been a war
The wars come & go
His father & father before him
They say it's in the nature of man
Walls peel off into even larger walls beneath
Our ruinous science
The passions are given to reason
The reasons swallowed by the wind
Sweet-eyed youth sink into the skull room of oblivion
The faces melt in their wax masks beneath
The burning sun

Behind us ashes
Before us a new destruction fires in the twilight

Today, I search for the beacon in your eyes.

Sara's Bedsheets: A Wedding Gift

NOEL KING

The sweetness of passion turned a corner
of cold pain. After being punctured by him
over the marriage, a diagnosis came.
She nurses her husband.

After weeks, he's too weak to do
anything and leaves her to life.

She tugs the bedsheets free;
on the clothesline, still seeing stains,
washes again, hot wash this time.
Back on the line the print
of death still laughs at her. Bleach!
Another wash. Iron. And at last she slips
under her sheets and takes the best
night's sleep she's had in years.

First, a Few Things Concerning the Poet

JASON RYBERG

First, it is essential
that the poet be
a failed "something else":

sculptor, guitar player, bridge builder,
astrologer, cosmetologist, mathematician, whatever,

something that sounded
like a "good idea" at the time.

(NOTE: anyone convinced
that writing poetry is a "good idea"
like the lightbulb was a good idea,
like penicillin was a good idea,
like peach pie with French vanilla
ice cream was a good idea
will one day make a fine mathematician,
literary critic, or iron worker, even.)

Poetry, like drag racing or black magic
or juggling knives, for that matter,
is rarely ever a "good idea."

Studies show that a poet is twice as likely
as a dentist and three times as likely
as a city commissioner to erupt into screaming fits
in the middle of a shopping mall,
a taut courtroom drama, or
an International House of Pancakes.

No, in fact, poetry is, to the shock
and dismay of those who would approach it
carelessly or attempt to feed it,
a half-starved and voracious
compulsion somewhere between
doodling in the margins of library books
and carving designs in your arm with a razor.

Poetry is a cosmic meta-psychic-al occurrence
somewhere between a fifty-gallon drum suddenly
coughing up flames in a vacant lot late one night
and a Grecian urn burning with wildflowers
on an unkempt inner-city grave.

Poetry comes in a deep, voice-like hum
somewhere between bee's wings
and whale song, thrumming and thrumming
at the base of the skull,

a voice calling out its pleas and directives
from the heart of the hive
and the depths of the sea,

a briny ghost's *basso profundo*
that you can never quite be sure
whether anyone else is hearing.

In fact, poetry is the confirmed poet's
dirty little secret,
like HAM radio,
fantasy baseball league,
a phone-sex gig,
or a good, solid heroin addiction.

Something the true devotee
(meaning here: *"one who has been turned"*)
wisely keeps hidden away (these days, especially)
on some grubby, candlelit altar, let's say,
at the back of a closet
or in the corner of a basement
or, better yet, locked in an old bomb shelter
out in the backyard.

And, while not widely known,
The Poet is, at the cellular level,
a type of rogue alchemist or depraved horticulturalist
trying tirelessly, against all common wisdom
and better judgment, to husband

monkeys and footballs,
dragons and freight trains,
flame jobs and blow jobs,
newspaper tigers and tinfoil unicorns,
donkeys and onions,

knowing full well that,
99 times out of 100,
he'll wind up holding an onion with big ears …

But still, none-the-less,
he or she must burn
the sacred Mexican Votive Candle of Prosperity
to the hope for that one piece of ass
that wrings tears from his eyes,
water from dirt,
gold from lead,
chicken salad from chicken shit,

life from a furious,
life-long struggle

with life.

Last Night—

DANA M. JERMAN

I stayed up until just after 3 a.m.

Read a short book at an all-night restaurant.

Not sure if my waitress had any teeth.

Everything else up and down the street was dark,
but the night still sparkled with orange lights
and new frost cold.

My breath was a cloud,
and a flag.

Dylan Thomas' Grave Letters

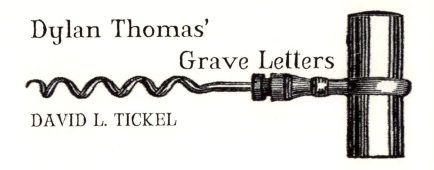

DAVID L. TICKEL

Some hottie
Loathed Composition I. I wrote
Papers for her.
One featured Jack Kerouac and
Jack Nitzsche, when I meant Friedrich Nietzsche.

I wrote a
Poym for
The Creative Writing professor:
"The dog gave his life for a
Small red ball." The professor didn't like that line,
But maybe
He didn't know too much about dogs.

Serve Me the Sky with a Big Slice of Lemon

J. BRADLEY

The Bushmills / ginger beer cocktail
simmers around the rocks bottoming
in our Jameson-labeled glasses;
we ignore the betrayal with every sip.

I smooth out the day from your back.
My teeth suggest we make revisions
to the banshee myth.

Along the Old Parade Routes

ANDREI GURUIANU

Occasional strangers resolved and serious about their fate
passing by a row of cramped boutiques
where the implements of unconditional gloom
were under lock and key and glimmering.
Even the mannequins struck modest poses.

And because this was an adults-only affair,
all of the children were kept behind guardrails and fences
with an obscured view of the procession.

I still remember the young woman in a tight-fitting dress
thumbing a cheap, plastic crucifix around her neck.

Said she spent her nights in a room above a street
of empty butcher shops and fortune tellers,
weeping alone in the shared silence of her God.

Years later she was found pointing a gun at a doll's head,
then her own.
The chamber full of blanks.

So this is what they didn't want us to see.
That it comes wearing black for the occasion,
always ready for a night out on the town.

The plump torturer and his debutante
holding hands and moving upwind through the crowd,
sneaking into after-hour cafés for a quick kiss
before settling down to a pattern of formalities.

The same familiar brick walls with the same old photographs
one memorized in grade school.
Evening meals presided over by a row of saints and criminals
rubbing shoulders above empty plates and worn-out sentiments.

The dinner never ending.

Roll Call

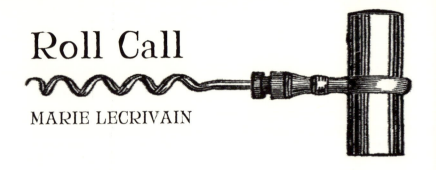

MARIE LECRIVAIN

I sit in a chair
with a wad of stuffing
pressed against my coccyx:
the result of many hours
spent by others before me,
who fidgeted with worry,
waiting, waiting, *waiting*...

I sip coffee, knit a potholder.
I lose at lotto scratchers
while I try to ignore
the *ABC* morning talk-show hosts
reminding housewives across America
that an $88 maxi dress
is affordable—to those who
reside in Upper Manhattan.
The procession of patients,
nurses, and X-Ray techs
starts to become a blur.
I watch one elderly woman
clad in Cancer Pink—
her scalp glistens
as she struggles out
of her chair—
be gently escorted
into the next room,
and the gray double doors
labeled *Mammography*
close silently behind her.
I hand tissues to
a blond mother-to-be
who quietly cries,
frustrated and confused
after repeatedly bludgeoned

with the question: *Do you have
a lump or a mass?* by a nurse
so steeped in her routine
she has no time to
contemplate
the casual cruelty
she skillfully wields.
I listen to names being called,
and notice the empty chairs
that echo those absent,
and wonder where they are,
how they're doing,
and why they're not
here ...

Any Similarities Between the Characters in This Purely Fictional Story and Actual Individuals Are Purely Coincidental

PHILL ARENSBERG

It was one of those perfect New York City summer nights. The cool of the evening had just begun to settle in and the humidity, previously so oppressive, was a comforting lushness in the air. Outside of our kitchen window, elms and oaks clustered around the brownstones and apartment buildings. The ever-present lion's roar of New York was there; running in counterpoint was the music box melodies of a lone Mr. Softee truck plying its way back and forth through the grid. We had a galley-style kitchen in our apartment. Small, tight, and intimate. It mushroomed out into a dining area where our battered table lived. The table was covered with two cats drowsily nosing the breeze, a tangle of *New York Times* sections, and our wine glasses. Brenda and I moved easily around each other in the small kitchen as we prepared our meal.

Mexican night. She toasted taco shells in the oven while I chopped and diced onions, peppers, and chilies for ceviche. It was perfect—one of those sweet, soft moments that you summon when things are cold or tense or dire. I remember Count Basie on the stereo, "Stomping at the Savoy." Negative spaces—between the piano and the orchestra, between Brenda and me in the kitchen. Comfortable yet charged with energy and passion.

Passion. When passion is given such a fertile, lush, luscious arena in which to loll and lounge, it will get antsy. It will get stir crazy, and, as the oppressive heat of July in the city lifts, it will grin its ape grin and start to stir the pot. I stirred. I stirred the bowl of chopped lime-soaked aromatics. I stirred in my jeans and T-shirt. Brenda was wearing a white skirt, loose and diaphanous, low on her hips. She swayed and bopped with the music. Her *FASHION SUCKS* T-shirt stretched across her breasts. I stirred. Passion grinned and turned up the volume. We had our backs to each other, she facing the stove, I facing the counter. I had just diced a deep green, glossy jalapeño and added it to my bowl. I started to mix gently and to knead, wiped my hands with a tea towel, and turned.

Brenda was grinning at me. She was grinning a grin that passion had lent her. And it worked. Well. I couldn't help but smile back at her. It was a perfect evening. We were young, safe, in love in New York. We kissed. My hands trailed to her hips. We kissed some more. Her hands cupped my face and played with my hair. My hands moved up, under her shirt, lifting, cupping, teasing. Her hands were like birds. Not fluttery and delicate, but like kingfishers: focused, dive-bombing toward my fly with intent and purpose. There was no fucking around. The skirt was next to go. I remembered she had bought it in Mexico, and, despite the heat of the place, I'm sure the skirt, raised in a strict Catholic country where propriety is paramount, could not be party to the porn that was about to go down in our kitchen. Ever chivalrous, my pants had departed, as well, no doubt to escort Brenda's skirt to a place of sanctity. I pictured them nestled together in a quiet church for vespers. But regardless of how demure our clothes were, we certainly had other plans. I stroked myself briefly, then saw to Brenda like John the Baptist and prepared the way.

Her hands slammed down on the counter, rattling the cookware. She looked over her shoulder at me, smiling, the all-American beauty wet dream dangerous curves ahead whipsmart .357 Teflon-coated Saturday night special liberal heartland taking what she wanted and giving back the same. And we moved together. And still Basie and his crew jumped and jived as twilight turned to dark. And it was perfect. The floor was cool and the night was spread out and we moved together. And then it got hot. And with that last sentence, I have abandoned metaphor. It was not porno hot or erotic hot. It was actually hot. I wasn't sure if I was imagining it or not, so, like a good soldier, I continued onward toward victory. Then, all uncertainty departed the situation as Brenda jumped forward and left me hanging.

"What the fuck?" To this day, I'm still not certain who yelled it, but we were both thinking it.

Our genitals had become completely coated with the oil from the jalapeño, inside and out. There is no small amount of personal insight you may gain from jumping around a tiny kitchen with your lover whose junk, like yours, is smeared with Mexican fire juice. I was in no position to appreciate truly the finer points of this insight because I was busy trying to wedge my pelvis into the sink.

Brenda was in much the same predicament, although it was apparent that she had a somewhat firmer grasp on the cause / effect symmetry of the moment. "You ASSHOLE! Why didn't you wash your hands?" This was delivered in something halfway between a yelp and a giggle.

By this point, I had moved to a prone position on the linoleum. My cock was still sweltering under the devastating onslaught of the fiery Latino pepper. Brenda was doing laps around the apartment, fanning her crotch with a magazine. This seemed like a good plan.

Dignity, often something we take for granted, can seem like a far-away shining city on the plains when you're wearing nothing but shoes and a T-shirt while playing tug of war with a copy of *Mirabella* so that you can fan your wang which had, by this point, turned the color of a flamingo. The air currents clearly were not working. In fact, both the fanning technique and the application of water had done nothing but exacerbate the situation. We once again found ourselves in the kitchen, pantsless with our junk on fire. I was at a loss and was trying to envision a life where "searing pain" would be the default state for penis.

Brenda grabbed onto the front of my shirt, twisted, and took a toupee's worth of chest hair with her. "Milk!" she yelled. I looked confused, but as I had basically caused this entire incident and had nothing as productive as "Milk!" to offer, I figured discretion should be my watchword, right after "Fuck, my dick is burning!"

Five minutes later, we were hanging out in the bathroom, while the cats quietly dined on broken taco shells shattered in our Crotch Fire dance. It was once again quiet and cool in the apartment. I stood leaning against the sink enjoying the feeling of the cool tile on my bare feet. Brenda sat next to me on the toilet. I reached out to lay a hand tenderly on her shoulder. My other hand loosely held a glass of milk in which my cock and balls lounged like retirees in a Palm Beach hot tub. Brenda tried not to snicker too much, as it tended to complicate the milk-soaked tampon she was currently enjoying.

"When I turn this into a short story," I asked, "where do you think I should say I got the idea?"

Brenda's response was instantaneous and vehement, "Other people's lives." It was perfect.

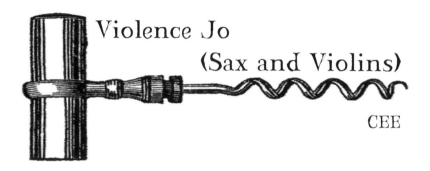

Violence Jo
(Sax and Violins)

CEE

To me, as an adolescent
Bad, Bad Leroy Brown
May as well have been a Cosby Kid
Like the wronged woman in "Dark Lady"
Wasn't a murderess
Just because she killed two people
But I felt Billy die, when he illadvisedly
Tried to be a hero
When just a few years before,
Billy Joe McAllister had jumped off into
Me, jumping to the funnies
I could feel Billy, though, the would-be hero
Being dead, unmourned,
Sitting in the local pizza joint
Sitting with two girls two years older
Than me
Either of whom I wanted to go home with
The vital, twain aspects of the lifeforce being
Siamese twins
They are,
Billy was dead, no real hero
I couldn't shake that empty cold
unless I got into some heat

Words made of flesh and memory

ALEX STOLIS

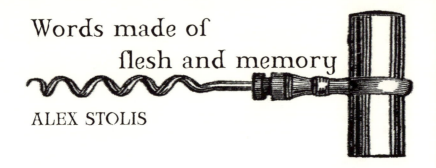

She tells me since she was a girl she liked to count: how many steps
to school or around the block, the freckles on her sister's face, leaves

on the tree outside her room. She gave up on the stars; what's the use
if you can't see them all. Today, she counts my sins, one by one, refuses

to tell the number; love by any other name, she says. She counted the days
until her father died. Mondays were pine needles and honey; Tuesdays

cinnamon; Wednesdays were candied apples and lemon. The days we
meet are Thursdays: the park is bright with the smell of rain and earth.

Together, we count each other: my hand, 2; her calf, 4; the mole on her
thigh is 7; we are whole and natural, smoothed-round and even.

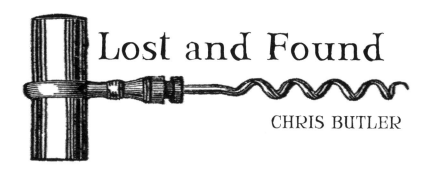

Lost and Found

CHRIS BUTLER

Every time my heart breaks, a few pieces go missing:
between the couch cushions, under the oriental rug, cuddling a dust
bunny in the vacuum's belly, inside of my shoe's sole, hiding in my other
pocket, locked in the vegetable crisper, buried beneath the egg shells and
coffee grounds in the trash, and around the lost and found.
Every time my heart breaks, I can't find them all.

How My SUV Helped Me

VICTOR SCHWARTZMAN

I liked being selfish
I liked fitting in
I loved our society
cashing in life coupons
The world was my big-box store

Sure, I didn't like breathing
when there were air quality warnings
or drinking the tap water
when toxic crap spilled into the reservoir again
but hell: into each life some acid rain must fall, eh?

Once in a while I felt bad we shipped crap
to countries with no environmental laws
but they're gonna buy them from someone
With the sales, my stocks soared
I bought a really cool SUV

But there is no justice in this world
The parking brake broke on my SUV
It rolled down the driveway and killed me
On the positive side
the tread marks made my forehead look
like my brow was furrowed from thinking

morning after halloween

NORMAL

a parade of 10-yr-old devils
& prepubic ancient witches
marched past the funeral
home & then on to the
village green

in the morning
a condom was found

sweating in the mud.

In a Gift of Stickers

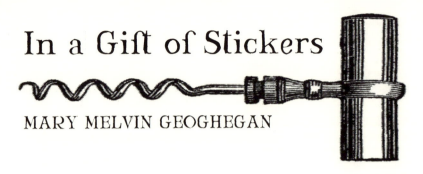

MARY MELVIN GEOGHEGAN

For Joan McBreen

Chagall arrived today—
in a booklet of stickers.
Almost in the same way years ago,
my father pulled out the artist
just as I was about to leave.
Flicking through—
I become his subject.
He invites me to choose a city,
color, century, and time of day.
On reflection, I tell him,
"Paint me in North County Dublin
in amongst the cowslips
sitting beside my brother
up in Kettle's field on a Sunday.
Our father and sisters down at the water
and our mother resting
on a cloud."

Yours

JARED A. CARNIE

Are you writing?
She says.

Sure am
He says.

They are twenty years married.
Unsatisfied.

What's it about?
She says.

You, he says,
This poem is about you.

She blushes
Smiles
And walks out.

My god,
He thinks,
I must start
Hiding my notebooks.

The History of an Odradek

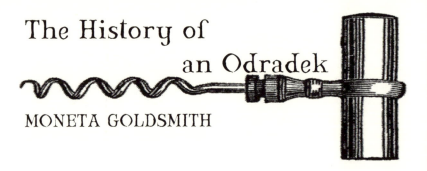

MONETA GOLDSMITH

After Franz Kafka

There I am standing at the bus stop unsure of my footing in this world, with not a single thing to say for myself even in the most casual direction, in this town, in this life, and there is this girl with fine-meshed lace and tendrils on the bench nearby (her hair is in tendrils that dance on her shoulder there); and there I am listening to the trees, not looking at the girl at all, just thinking about the trees, about their private lives and losses, thinking about their nightly whispering and their ancient tremors, all the things that trees might do and complain about, the vandalism and the accidental tattoos that lovers carve into their loving bark, those kinds of things that cover up the greatest of man and man's ambitions, and so I am standing there, a man apart, a young old man listening stupidly to the trees in their dull dreams, imagining their fear of breaking the silence, a silence of whispers, or of words, a silence that even the trees fail to admit, and so I am standing there picturing all this when the girl sitting on the bench nearby, a girl no older than sixteen years old, she lurches over her side of the bench she's been sitting on and she rolls onto the concrete there; she rolls and rolls until she vomits all over one side of the bus booth and there I am hearing myself laughing as she vomits right on my shoe there and I just laugh and laugh like a man who doesn't have any lungs, and so the girl looks at me, the girl sitting there on the asphalt ground, she just looks at me like an abused puppy, and all the while I'm laughing, laughing terribly, laughing like a man without any lungs, right on the spot where the girl has just vomited a moment ago; and so the girl rolls back, she rolls slowly, like her vomit has now been rolling far down into the gutter there, as if her lungs were falling out along with it, collecting a thick mud as robust as tendrils, settling over the bench and covering up the curb and the bus is about to arrive now, and there she is practically rolling down into the street until the bus is there, and until the girl and me and the trees and everything else comes to a stop.

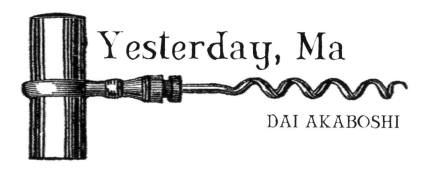

Yesterday, Ma

DAI AKABOSHI

Yesterday,
it became complete ash, sleeping under the ground—
her body, I mean. She died three days ago in the hospital.
That was the worst gift she's ever given for my birthday—
my thoughts as I passed a handkerchief to her crying granddaughter.

2 months ago,
her doctor told my wife and me that Ma didn't have much time for us.
In 3 or 4 days, she could be gone forever. That's what he confirmed,
in his neat office with his professional, hopeless smile.

A half-year ago,
because of her age and her body getting weaker,
her sickness grew stronger than her body could keep up with,
one more surgery, but still she half-smiled for us,
fighting against it. I, helpless. Her skinny wrinkled arms,
holding her cold hand; she could barely eat.

One year ago,
the second surgery, waiting and waiting, the odor of the hospital,
with a hint of piss and shit and unfavorable medicine kicking in,
increased my nerve, circled around purposelessly,
while my daughter, Sarah, slept, her head on her mother's lap.

Three years ago,
she told us that she didn't feel well. We took her to the hospital.
We were expecting nothing heavy. A week later,
the doctor speaking the hospital language to my wife and me,
my ears didn't buy his words. "Pancreatic cancer." I swallowed bile.
That next day, there she was. "Everything is going to be all right, Ma,"
my hands trembling. At night, the thought was too powerful to handle;
I cried on my wife's shoulder.
"Everything is going to be all right, darling,"
said she, petting my back.

Seven years ago,
my old man passed away in a car accident.
A stupid young kid ran over him and.
That was that. He was gone.
We remained calm and let days cure us. By then, Ma was lonely,
so we invited her to live with us. She did; the same year,
she met her granddaughter. Through the difficulty,
she found happiness.

Thirteen years ago,
having a little argument with Ma about me not going to college,
though I did in the end. Back then, my grades were exceptionally good,
but I couldn't see myself going to study more.
Ma never raised her voice, but she said, "You should go to college,
or someday, you may regret it."
I met my wife during those college years.

Twenty or twenty-five years ago,
Ma, you were always at home, waiting for me after school.
Asking me what I did, what I learned,
where I got scars and bruises from.
Snacks and juice were always prepared.
Hugged me every time you were proud of me
or when I was down. I didn't appreciate you
as much as I should have.

Thirty-nine years ago,
you spent exactly 8 months and 26 days, carrying a little one
inside you, thinking about names: Mark, like your husband
or Andy, like my grandfather, but you named me Dan, out of nowhere.
Two days of holding my father's hand and pushing, and I was born.
I made you my ... from that day you were ...
until yesterday, no, even now, and until I die,
you're still my mother.

Jesus didn't wash his own feet

NOEL KING

Asking why you don't wash
your feet before going to bed,
you told me you didn't care.
All day you'd swept around
on the beach, in the caravan park,
on the dirt tracks, the sandhills,
going to the shop for ice creams
and now, after fourteen hours of fun,
you get into your nightie and into bed with filthy feet.

I bathe mine in warm water and soap in a plastic pan
we keep under the sink. *That's just sissy,* you say
and jump into that borrowed sleeping bag without a care.

I roll the zip down on my bag and climb in; you are on your own
bunk, start to lip a prayer, let your dark hair
fall on the day cushions with pink pillow-covers.
Soon you are snoring softly, and I dream of you
Mary Magdalene-like washing my feet,
like a good love only could, but that would be a sin
as you—lovely and all as you are—are my cousin.

In the morning we will jump into the sea
again before breakfast, paddle across the water.

No Words Required

BRIAN C. FELDER

My littlest cousin, Sonja,
sleeps quietly upon my chest,
her tiny hands clutching a fold of my neck
as if I were her blanket.
We are, after a fashion, conversing,
my heart telling hers
all it needs to know for now:
that she is loved and that she is safe.
Her month-old heart,
beating peacefully against mine,
seems to understand
and a pact is struck between us.
It is a perfect moment,
as the beginning of all love affairs are,
one that needs no language.

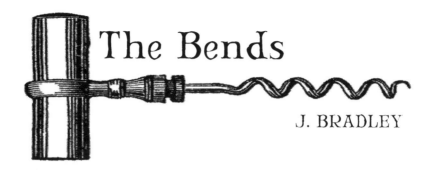

The Bends

J. BRADLEY

"Where do we go from here," she asked. Chlorine
stained the needle of my finger pointing
at the adjacent bathroom door. On the sink,
I unwrapped her, ignoring the tea leaves
of her bikini on the tile, grateful
for her trained silence.

                    My mother swelled, winked
when I brought Callie home, counted with ease
the mistakes we'd make.

                    After the condom
broke during our second time, my baptism
soured; I offered my fingers instead,
knelt on carpet, wool, wood, and laminate.

If I had read the tea leaves, tracked which way
the water pooling in the tile ran toward,
I would have learned faster not to need you.

Barbie Wonders about Buying a Coffin

LYN LIFSHIN

if she'll need one,
not that these
plastic boxes she's
in so long on a
shelf aren't like
being buried in a
toy box under eaves,
freezing in winter,
scorched by June.
She wonders if they
will bury her in a
ballerina costume,
a rodeo suit, if
they'll shave her
hair or braid it.
Just because she's
empty doesn't mean
she doesn't care. Or
that her velvet or
tulle, even her under
pants have been stripped
from her and she was
left nude as some
one in the camps
about to march into
gas, doesn't mean
she doesn't want
to know if she'll go
with one of her
many scarves around
her, a la Isadora.

Or if Ken, supposing
she's eying a Ricky
or P. T. or Alan,
even trying Christie,
rages in, beans her
with his boogie board,
strangles her with
the ropes of his
Hawaiian Fun hammock
or poisons her with
cyanide in soda
from the All-American
store, runs her over
in a remote-control
Corvette and leaves
her in the trunk
with nothing to wear
for this last stop

Pseudo-Aster

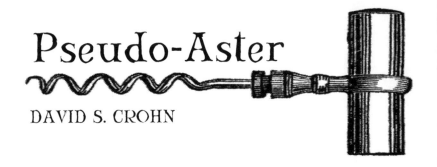

DAVID S. CROHN

Pa had been dead a few days when I returned home after a long journey through the Territories. The screen door was torn from the hinges and tossed into the yard, the front door broken open, an angry patch of splintered wood and scratched metal where the latch used to be. Above the familiar rhythm of creaks and groans rising from the floor, I heard flies droning amidst the smell of fresh rot. "Ma," I said. Nothing. Then, "Father." Finally, "Aster." The sound grew louder as I approached the kitchen.

Father was splayed facedown on the linoleum, the entire top of his skull broken, its contents feeding the mist of flies. Footprints streaked the blood across the linoleum in uneven slips and fits. The prints led from the body to the back door of the kitchen. Out the door, down the steps, and into the backyard, where I found an Aster, digging. The digger had his mop of hair, his gray eyes, my brother's unmistakable build—the broad shoulders leveled below a too-small head. I recognized the T-shirt, faded-iron camo with a wheat-brown patch just beneath the collar Mother sewed in after I had torn it during a childhood wrestle. Only it was not Aster. The person recognized me.

"Hello, Lumpy," said the digger, dumping a shovelful of wet earth onto a growing mound. A spade was thrust into the ground beside them.

"Who ... the fuck ..." I said.

"Lumpy. That's no way to speak." The voice failed at being stern, was instead disconsolate, defeated.

"Don't call me that," I said.

The pseudo-Aster paused and looked at me, shoulders slumped. Then, after a moment, resumed the chore.

"What have you done?" I said, because I really didn't know. The hole in the ground was pulling everything into its own diminishing reality, perpetuating its own emptiness.

The pseudo-Aster's face frowned and furrowed. I had perturbed this person, had come to his / her fashion late and empty-handed.

"You could help, you know," said the Pseudo-Aster in a voice now like white linen, tapping the wooden handle of the spade with the wooden handle of the shovel. The spade should have fallen over but didn't. "You think this is for my health?" She spoke from under her breath or the side of her mouth now, and dug. "Ungrateful." Stab. Lift, dump. "Good-for-nothing." Stab, lift—

"Stop. You'll hurt yourself," I said, and went to the spade.

The Knock on the Door

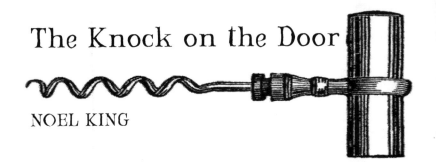

NOEL KING

... is dead in water ...
the gardaí say.

My daughter who
from her mother's death waters
    came in my life:
    changing her nappies,
    dressing her the first five years,
    school-running, films, birthday parties, horse-trekking,
    Enid Blyton's packed with my Grisham's for holidays,
    keeping up with keeping up with the Spice Girls, Steps
    and Boyzone, buying her her first legal Bacardi Breezer
    to celebrate the Leaving Cert. results,
    waving after the college train,
    meeting that homing train
    for weekends to drive her here and there,
    anywhere, weekend after weekend,
until this boyfriend I've never met,
this boyfriend with the boat,
this weekend.

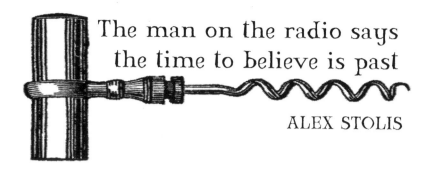

The man on the radio says the time to believe is past

ALEX STOLIS

In this dream you were gone. There was a country scene: quiet yellow fields, a faded red barn, water; a lake or a stream, a shade tree where we fucked. There was a city scene: an upscale coffee shop, a bus shelter in winter, a second-hand bookstore, parking lot of your kids' school. There you weren't. There wasn't a word, no soundtrack or marks to hit. You didn't say you were leaving, didn't say you were coming back. There was no letter exchange or last chance. In this dream I made every one of your scars mine, mapped every crease, every white line. Traced them with my finger and waited for you; felt the earth shiver under the weight of silence.

Tatau

JENNIFER LEEPER

Everything on the old Tahitian's body was 123 years old, thought the tattooist. He tapped along the man's inner and outer arm flesh to determine its resiliency and thickness. His own 75-year-old Polynesian genetics had lightly browned his limbs to the same shade as the ancient man before him, but they had also thinned his aging skin so that it was much less reliable in its composition than the other man's. The tattooist was like an impressive boulder, shaped by time and place, powerful in motion or in its lack thereof, but he was nothing then, sitting beside a mountain that no longer moved, but everything else moved around it, even time itself.

This was the old man called Keko, in a southeastern slice of Tahiti where he had outlived two wives and all three of his children. Keko was the oldest living being, according to several reputed Western sources. Beyond the prowess of his age, his blood that would soon mix with ink was of a royal vigor, donated from kings and queens of the water dynasties of Oceania where men once dove as elegantly as dolphins for pearls, and darkly exotic women lured European adventurers and artists alike to their island nations.

Keko knew he was dying, and with no vices to speak of other than a small corncob tobacco pipe that he had smoked for 10 of his 11 decades, he only requested a *tatau*, old Samoan for tattoo, before his death. He asked for Aikani, the oldest tattooist in Polynesia, to memorialize the scenes of his life on his body.

"My mother was a Tahitian princess who ran away with a pearl diver who was part Samoan and part merman. No, he was Hawaiian, too. So, I claim my line from the northern waters, as well." Keko's eyes squinted, tiny smiling wrinkles creasing his wide-cheekboned face. His long, white hair was braided down his back, but it was censored from view as he lay on a homemade surfboard that had plunged often into the raging cold cauldron of surf that he happily confronted as one of a thousand muscular primitives dotting a Tahitian coastline a century before. He spoke *Tuamotu* first, but to Aikani, a Hawaiian, he offered a choppy English.

"Your blood must be highborn to feed your skin so well at your age. Even I'm too old anymore for the ink." Aikani's own face rippled throughout with smiling wrinkles.

He began tracing the life of Keko across his chest and arms, in nimble strokes, following this painless rehearsal with pain-filled, metallic pricks. Aikani sweated out images of Keko's life of diving for black-lipped oyster pearls and finally meeting his grandfather, the last true king of Tahiti. His eyes never left his own unraveling of the man until, at last, he felt as if the Pacific itself had pulled him under. It was the eyes of Keko, these two oceans of death, swimming with a final peace.

Sal Mineo

DAVID L. TICKEL

Was murdered in
My basement bedroom.

My family
Had
Recently moved from

Nearby Levittown (where there were
Streetlights) to

A well-to-do,
Racist neighborhood, where
I

Accidentally first heard
Cale's "Fear Is a Man's Best Friend."

But I was only scared of
Girls

Something Out There

MARY MELVIN GEOGHEGAN

from the window
of the back bedroom in Abbeycartron
across the football pitch
an early Spring evening
its afterbirth and light
just delivered.

Madame Laveau, Fortune Teller and Police Psychic, Falls off the Wagon with a Resounding Thud

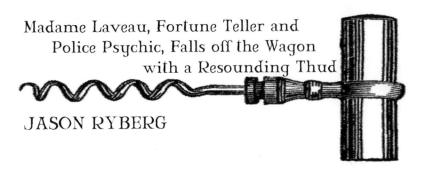

JASON RYBERG

I see a dark and cluttered curiosities shop
overflowing with old tuxedos and fancy combs,
snuff boxes and china dolls,
big belt buckles and giggling garden gnomes,
books and magazines and postcards
from places that no longer exist,
(to people who've been gone for decades).

I see an ominous gothic architecture
full of monstrous ideas (stuffed
and mounted, but still not quite dead).

I see an old, rundown Vaudeville theater
wherein old, rundown drunks
watch naked emotions writhe
and gyrate upon a spotlit stage.

I see leaves falling on the surface of a pond:
fish bones, beer bottles, rowboats, and
old dreams asleep on the cold, muddy bottom.

I see a plow mule, trapped and maddened,
in the ballroom of an abandoned antebellum mansion,
and a furious black thunderstorm (with lightning
in its hair) pounding and pounding at the front door,
demanding an offering of spare change
and Châteauneuf-du-Pape.

I see a sailor in a bar,
drinking gin and playing gin rummy
(secretly pining for his past life as a barn swallow),
and a tailor's dummy standing in the corner
of a tiny room, just upstairs from the bar;
the soles of somebody's shoes
showing from beneath the bed,
something sinister or ridiculous
(or both) about to happen.

I see a man walking down a dark street,
unable to sleep without his nightly dosage
of Ellington's *Indigos* or Gould's *Variations*.

His heart is a wasp's nest laboring
earnestly to make honey.

His head is a hotel kitchen
full of screaming Greeks and Mexicans and Slavs,
and one lost and rather simple-looking white boy.

The man has stooped to pick something up
from the street corner, an important-looking key
on a bright red string,
a Christmas ornament, almost,
in its shining, ornate delicacy.

Though he will later misplace it
somewhere foolishly obvious
during some minor misadventure,
nevertheless, it will continue to lead him
in ever-widening and shrinking circles
like an ill-advised idea or broken diving rod,

most likely for the rest of his life.

Endeavour

MARIE LECRIVAIN

"Touch has a memory."
—John Keats

Dedicated to John Whiteside Parsons

We're here to see *Endeavour*,
which, like Chavez or Lenin,
has been laid out in state.

The line of people winds
through the hangar like a snake
that warms itself under the sun,

and the smiles on our faces
widen in anticipation as we
draw closer to the space shuttle,

what we'd assumed would be
the first in a long line
of great galactic buses

that would carry us to the stars
and back ... but, alas, that is
not to be, as long as those

in power refuse to dream.
I come within a few feet
of *Endeavour's* mighty lines;

I can see why space travel
is still alive in the hearts
of the hopeful. I lift my hand

overhead, stroke the roughened
edges of scorched tiles, the blasted
sides that mark the history

of re-entry to our lonely planet
by the alchemical fires of space,
and rendered its passengers

into something finer, more
hallowed than human. How
badly I yearn to connect

with this current, the ultimate
wish for us all: to be more
than our mere shells, so close
to touch, and just out of reach.

Life Partners

VICTOR SCHWARTZMAN

Lived with that woman thirty years
every hour of which she had work for me
Never talks until I start something
Always has to get her way
Always has to be right
I love her
This is what love is

Lived with that man thirty years
most of them he sat, nothing to do
I talked because of the silences
Always has to get his way
Always has to be right
I love him
This is what love is

Lived with my parents eighteen years
We did a lot despite their arguments
Their words, weapons and caresses
Both have to get their own way
Both have to be right
I love them but
I hope this isn't what love is

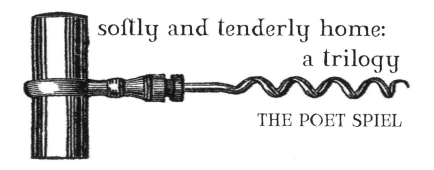

softly and tenderly home: a trilogy

THE POET SPIEL

the homecoming book 1

how she can windex the glass
how she can be so meticulous
    as she polishes the silver rosettes on its
    onyx frame with a toothbrush and toothpaste
    at the start of each day
but she can never create a more perfect picture

how her mouth is stretched so wide
how the heat of his finger is pressed onto her
    tongue
his knuckle gobbed with orange-scented
    yellow frosting nearly jamming her nostrils
her impulse to gag then giggle on sugar and joy

her ecstasy in capturing him
how all of this is contained
    in the 8x10 walmart photo frame

the homecoming book 2

how her little ones are spit images
    of the man with his finger down her throat
how she teases them to get her breasts sticky
    with all the purple kool-aid and mud
    they can paint on her
how she's frantic as she whips
    yellow frosting into the night
    when the kiddies wake screaming:
    why can't he stick with us
    when he gets to come home

how she traces her face in the bedroom mirror
    with the orange lipstick
    he said he liked in high school
how she fills in her mouth lines
    with the sugar taste of his finger
but the mouth is not gracious
    and she hears only her self as she weeps

the homecoming *book 3*

how the troops return minus one
    sometimes two or more somehow they return
each tour of duty he's made it back home
    respiring through his tongue like a spent dog

he gets smacked with wet cheers and balloons
but he cannot recall those who greet him
he does not trust hands that grope him
the blare of the band spooks him
how eyes in the back of his head
    weigh each twitch in the ruckus
but he doesn't know which way is home

how his triggerbrain is cocked by the least likely shock
    of sugary goo smeared on a doorknob
    or a kid's tricycle tire limping low on air
how he freaks at the pop of the cork
    on a bottle of homecoming champagne

how *he* is not his name

the homecoming *book 4*

how his coming home seems forever
how could anyone know how anxious she's been
how her mother will tend the children for the night
how she's had her nails done orange
    same orange as her lips
had her legs waxed glassy
had her hair streaked sexy
then cleansed herself

how she opens her legs like a V for victory
how she lures his triggerfinger down there
but his finger is so clumsy so frigid and estranged
how she can't even tease him
    to press it against her tongue
how he just wants to do another line of coke
    and another and another
she doesn't know where he gets it
does not know why he seems so removed

how she sees her self as a cubist still life
    framed in that same goddamn mirror

the homecoming book 5

how they come to terms to meet
    in a busy public place the walmart lunchroom
    where no one will notice them
where security guards will safe-watch them
they agree no weapons
    not even a his or hers fingernail file
how they will talk it out *right now*
    while he's on homeground

how she's frosted her bruises
    with a neutral foundation
how the kiddies tag along to protect her
so she buys each of them
    a dollar toy one hotdog and one small coke
but they stick thick to *his* thighs
    same as the icing on the wedding cake
    in her 8x10 frame
how they beg him:
    please daddy please stay inside
    our sleeping bags on top of us
    so the bad guys from where you go
    won't blow our heads off like on tv

but it's like he does not know them
he does not know her
how he says they have nothing to say
    now that all of them are here
    and his job is over there
how he's never been trained
    to be a lover or daddy
how what he's been trained to do best
    is what he does best

how his triggerbrain is cocked
how his fingers become coarse and rigid
    as they approach her throat
how she goes down easy
    barely a gurgle
how security guards pry the children from his legs
then mop mustard and catsup smears
    from their little faces

how these guards text management's permission
    to rush the little ones from this scene
    before hordes of saturday morning shoppers
    turn hysterical bringing shame to the face
    of this new south-side walmart
    built near the military base
    for the convenience of troops and
    their wait-at-home loved ones

    returnee: seven days *(softly and tenderly home)*

as troops hit homebase
    the anxious wife crushes her dumbstruck soldierboy
    with hits of gladness and hearts of helium
through glassy eyes like eyes she's never known
    he hits her back with sporadic jerks of unfamiliarity
her lips hit his teeth so hard
    his gums bleed onto the whimpering baby's throat

his first day home he hits the fridge hits the bottle
    hits the couch and hollers at tv hosts all day

he hits the dog with the bottle on his second day home
the dog nips a chunk out of his ear

on his third day he hits the ceiling
    and knocks plaster into the baby's crib
the baby stops crying

fourth day he hits the wife in her belly and shouts
    why should he give a shit she got knocked up
    when he last deployed

his fifth day home he hits the tv with her lace-up spikes
    then shreds every last credit card
    in her snazzy-ass designer purse

he hits the baby for stinking his fatigues on day six
he shakes the little shit into fearsome awe
then he hits a massive gap through her kitchen wall
    to get the forever fuck
    out of there

seventh day he hits the streets
    street by street casualty by casualty
    till he connives his way back
    into sanctioned combat

where lawlessness is law

it almost makes sense (softly and tenderly home)

bearing too much gear for his frame
    this dedicated kid turned blue and broke rank
    during his last line-up when the platoon sergeant
    addressed his troops as *ladies*

how the kid's auntie ivy had it figured
    he'd been shipped back home because she prayed
    for one more thanksgiving with him
    before jesus tenderly called her home

he appeared at her kitchen window
    with a stickmatch gripped between his teeth
    wearing a misfit ash-gray t-shirt announcing:
    Property of U.S. Government
more gaunt than when he deployed
complaining of sand in his ears
he yanked a few extra matches from his hip pocket
and struck fire against her screen door

he asked about the mothballed black dress
    frankie martinez'd challenged him to doll up in
    when they were eight playing halloween in the attic

                                    (but frankie'd humiliated him
                                        when he tagged him *girlie boy*
                                    in ivy's grandmother's best dress
                                  silky so pretty black like the attic)

he asked was the dress still stashed in that musty box
    that best black dress
that dress gave the boy lineage
so he carried a photo of it to prove where he came from

how ivy recalled when he was fifteen he'd come sobbing
    because frankie dared him
    to *nail delia johnson's rose*
but he'd gone limp so frankie did delia instead
all the kids never stopped talking

ivy never stopped trying to spark the heart
    of the lost boy
assuring him her grandmother wore that dress
    at the sacred site of her own WWI hero
assuring him he could become a better man
    than frankie martinez
he could burn his own path
like a pioneer

                                    (she never learned he'd tried the burn
                                when he challenged his sergeant's slur
                              with a hot pass at him then got kicked home
                        wearing the sergeant's cast-off shirt bearing the lie
                                    and harboring his plan)

but ivy got a looming in the hairs of her nostrils
it wasn't smoke from turkey gravy spilt on her burner
it reminded her of burning flesh in the camps of WWII

so she shouted *the turkey is hot the yams're ready*
    but the boy didn't come to table

he'd ditched his ash shirt and a few extra stickmatches
    up the stairs to the attic

it took her nearly five minutes of stoop labor
    up those two flights of smoky steps
then thoughtful hesitation before gaining
    courage to push the hot attic door

The Photographer

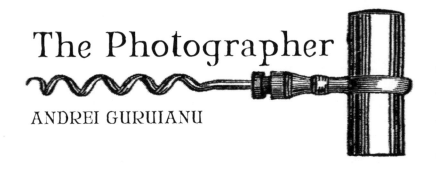

ANDREI GURUIANU

He'd stopped photographing landscapes almost as soon as he had begun. In recent years, he has stopped photographing anyone. We would walk around the city for hours, his camera swinging from its noose by his side. It was always at the ready, but he would never lift it to his eyes and tell you to hold still.

"An artist has a single job, to bring something to life. But how do you give life to something that hasn't died yet?"

He used to say such things when we first met. Part of what attracted me to him, I guess: the mind of an eccentric who could still tie his shoelaces and match his socks.

"I don't think most people think of it quite so literally," I remember saying once.

"Is there any other way?" It was his only reply.

Slowly, the walls of his studio became bare. He either sold most of his work or gave away what he couldn't sell. He stopped spending time in his darkroom. Instead, he pored over newspapers looking for garage sales, yard sales, estate sales, anyone moving out of town. He circled them in thick black marker, then made a list with addresses and phone numbers arranged by upcoming dates. That's how he spent most of his weekends, going from one sale to another, sometimes stopping at an antique store if there was one along the way. He had a single question when he got there: do you have any old photographs?

Anything would do, but he preferred those people looking to unload entire shoeboxes of memories. Something a distant aunt or recently deceased grandmother kept away in a dusty attic, under the bed, or in a corner of a wardrobe. If they had any, he would buy the entire box.

At home he would spend hours mulling over them, making piles. The children in one pile, and the adults in another pile. As soon as a batch was sorted this way, he would summarily toss the pile with the adults in the garbage. Hundreds of images. From one dark corner to another.

The rest of the photographs he scrutinized more closely. He would turn them over and read their inscriptions: names, places, salutations, dates. It didn't matter so much when and where the pictures were taken or who they were. He wanted to know when the photographs stopped being taken. *William _____, 1923-1929.* Or anything with the words: *In Loving Memory.*

Those photographs, maybe one or two out of a hundred, he held on to. And when we would go on our walks around the city, he would bring along his camera and those photographs.

"Think about it," he'd say. "What's one thing you wish you did when you were little that you never got to do?"

"Oh, I don't know. I can't remember."

"C'mon, c'mon," he'd press. "There has to be something you really wanted to do but never had the chance."

"The Empire State Building, I guess. I've lived my whole life in this city, and I still have never been to the top of the Empire State Building. Can you believe that?"

And without a second thought, he would turn and head in the direction of whatever place or thing went through my head that day. Other times, he would follow his own whims and not speak a word until we got to whatever it was that had materialized in his head. Once there, he would take out his set of old photographs and flip through them, selecting the one he felt most appropriate. He would prop it up against a railing, the skyline opening up beyond, or the lights of a rollercoaster causing multicolored streaks against the darkness. Sometimes, the picture lay simply in a field in Central Park, on a bench, on a seat in an old movie theater, the film rolling through the starry dust above our heads.

When the image was lined up just right, he would snap a shot and pick up the old photograph and put it away at the back of the pile. And in each of the photographs, as he was looking through the viewfinder and I was looking at him looking at them, the eyes and faces of those children would stare back at us from among blades of grass or leaning on a park swing on a summer afternoon.

"Well, what did you think of the Empire State Building?" he would ask. "Billy here looked like he had a good time; don't you think?" and he would pat his side pocket with the photographs.

Story of living on a fault line

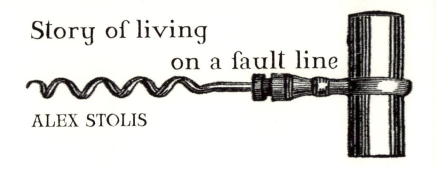

ALEX STOLIS

The day before the earthquake, she was drinking red wine,
remembering the first time, knowing how easy it is to confuse
wine for blood, blood for love, love for suffering. She knows
redemption is as simple as that mark on the wall under her
picture of Paris, the one she took in '99. She fell in love with
a man reading a book. He was sitting near Édith Piaf's grave;
she imagined him as English. She falls in love easily, at least
four times a week: on the bus, in line at the bank, twice at
the library. She knows what she cannot see, makes a toast:
to the flit of wings and the buzz of leaves in an autumn wind.
She remembers everything, how the world became rock and sky,
quartz and pyrite, how her name, on his lips, became weightless.

Just Weeks

LYN LIFSHIN

Just weeks before my mother's birthday, I
    wear the flesh-pink rhinestone barrette.
Too often I look backward from where I'm going.
I think of women who feel guilty not grieving as much
    after a year.
My blue couch is so much like my mother's.

Too often, I look backward, at loss.
Almost May, the middle name they gave her, sorry
    she wasn't a boy.
My blue couch, color of the dark one we curled on.
We could hear Otter Falls, the voices from Main Street.

May in 4 days. Frieda May, not the boy
    they hoped for.
After 65, she found the 28th wasn't her birthday.
Otter Falls and the traffic on Main Street blurred so much.
But not her father's disappointment on May 25th.

After 65, she found out they hadn't hurried to register
    her birth date, waited 3 days.
Even before she knew, she wanted girls she could
    shower with love,
wanted to make up for her father's cruel disappointment.
She named me Rosalyn for my rosebud mouth
    and because it sounded like a name for an actress.

Even before she knew her birthday was so disappointing
    that it wasn't reported for days,
she wanted girls.
She named me Rosalyn Diane, a name good for
    the theater.
"Performing daily," the birth announcement said.

She wanted girls,
named her second daughter Joy, hoping she
        would bring that.
My "performances daily" were what she
        looked forward to the rest of her life.

Author
BIOGRAPHIES

Dai Akaboshi
[Astoria, New York] is an experimental writer from Japan. He writes prose / poetry pieces, short screenplays, and so forth. He is never a blogger. He is never an essayist. He wasn't a chief editor. He is simply an aspiring writer. He strongly thinks English is the best language for literature, and hopefully he can be a part of the community. [pages 70, 99]

Phill Arensberg
[Seattle, Washington] hails from Albany, New York, graduated from Connecticut College with a BA in English literature, and attended the conservatory program at Chicago's Second City. He is the coauthor of the serialized radio play, *Who Killed Mysterioso*, as well as the creator of five improvised plays. Phill is an avid improviser, performing with Comedy Sportz and Boom Chicago, and he's also authored the narration of the documentary, *The Albany Mummies*. Currently, he lives in Seattle with his amazing wife, Holly, and their cat, Haroun. [page 88]

J. Bradley
[Orlando, Florida] is the author of the graphic poetry collection, *The Bones of Us* (YesYes Books, 2014), with art by Adam Scott Mazer. His chapbook, *Neil*, won Five [Quarterly]'s 2015 e-Chapbook Contest for Fiction. He is an MFA in Creative Writing candidate at Lindenwood University and runs the Central Florida-based reading series / chapbook publisher There Will Be Words. [pages 55, 83, 103]

Chris Butler
[Danielson, Connecticut] is a twentysomething starving artist. His latest chapbook in his Poems of Pain Series, *Bummer*, was published by Scars Publications. He is also the coeditor of the literary journal, *The Beatnik Cowboy*. [beatnikcowboy.com] [pages 60, 93]

Jared A. Carnie
[Sheffield, England] was awarded a New North Poets award at the Northern Writers Awards in 2015. His debut novel, *Waves*, is available through Urbane Publications. [jaredacarnie.com] [pages 19, 72, 97]

Kevin Catalano
[Gillette, New Jersey] is the author of the novel, *Where the Sun Shines Out* (Skyhorse, 2017). His writing has appeared in *PANK*, *Fanzine*, *Gargoyle Magazine*, *storySouth*, and other outlets, including being anthologized in *Surreal South* and *Fiddleblack*. He teaches at Rutgers University-Newark, and lives in New Jersey with his wife and two kids. [kevincatalano.com] [page 64]

CEE
[Normal, Illinois] is the author of 27 chapbooks, holds a Pushcart nomination, saw publishing of over 1,000 poems and a regular column, all in the past decade. He fails to see what else he's expected to do. It's not like he ever got that flying DeLorean. [pages 17, 67, 91]

Seth Clabough
[Charlottesville, Virginia, and Hatteras Island, North Carolina] is a fiction writer, poet, scholar, and author of the novel, *All Things Await*. His recent writing appears in the anthologies *Hearing Voices* (Kingston University Press) and *Transatlantic* (Ocean Media Books), and in *Nanoism*, *storySouth*, *Litro Magazine*, *The Chronicle of Higher Education*, and numerous other places. [sethclabough.com] [page 74]

David S. Crohn
[New York City, New York] is an MFA student and English teacher at the City College of New York. His work can be found in *Down and Out Magazine*, *Apocrypha and Abstractions*, and elsewhere. His outlook tends toward a moderate to high faith in visible signs of the invisible order. [pages 14, 56, 106]

Kelly Jean Egan
[San Francisco, California] received her MFA in Poetry at Saint Mary's College in Moraga, California. She also studied Spanish and generally obsesses about language. She likes to visit small towns. Her poetry has appeared in *Eunoia Review*, *Spry*, and *In Stereo Press*. [kellyjeanegan.com] [page 58]

Jonathon Engels
[Always Traveling] studied at Louisiana State University and received an MFA from the University of Memphis. He taught English abroad for

nearly a decade, during which time he traveled extensively and began writing travel articles and memoirs. He is currently on the mastheads of *Transitions Abroad*, *Green Global Travel*, and *Panorama: The Journal of Intelligent Travel*. He also writes regularly for *Permaculture News* and *One Green Planet*. [page 20]

Brian C. Felder
[Milford, Delaware] is a purveyor of fine poetry since 1969 and is delighted to be making his first appearance in *Poiesis Review*. Other significant publishing credits include *The Humanist*, *Atlanta Review*, *Mas Tequila Review*, *Chiron Review*, *Owen Wister Review*, *Connecticut River Review*, *Iconoclast*, and *Little Balkans Review*. [pages 13, 73, 102]

Mary Melvin Geoghegan
[Ireland] has five collections of poetry published. Her current, *As Moon and Mother Collide* (2018), was published with Salmon Poetry, Ireland. Her work has been published widely, including in the Hodges Figgis 250th Anthology, *Poetry Ireland Review*, *The Sunday Times*, *Cyphers*, *The Moth*, *The Stinging Fly*, *The Stony Thursday Book*, *Crannóg*, *Skylight 47*, and others. She was shortlisted in 2017 for the Fish Poetry Award and won the Longford Festival Award for poetry in 2013. [pages 16, 69, 96, 113]

Kathy Gilbert
[Daly City, California] is an award-winning poet and commissioned playwright. She received an MFA in Creative Writing / Poetry in 2013, and she previously had a career in public transit operations. Kathy currently tutors in a public school and loves yoga, swimming, and reading. [is.gd/kathygilbert] [page 52]

Moneta Goldsmith
[Santa Monica, California] has been published both in print and online in *Sparkle & Blink*, *Iron Horse Review*, and *Best New Writing* (2014). He is a Pushcart nominee, a Grand Prize winner of The Spark Anthology Annual Poetry Contest, and a Finalist for the Gover Prize in flash fiction. He is also the cofounder of the reading series and pataphysical litmag, *When in Drought*. [page 98]

Andrei Guruianu
[New York] writes work that often explores such topics as memory and forgetting, and the ability of place to shape personal and collective histories. He currently teaches in the Expository Writing Program at New York University. [andreiguruianu.com] [pages 59, 84, 126]

Dana M. Jerman
[Chicago, Illinois] was born in the dawn of a western Pennsylvania spring and has written for several print and online publications, including *Big River Review*, *AfterHours*, *The Capitola Review*, and *Theurgy Magazine* in the U.K. Her chapbook of poetry and illustrations, *Sins in Good Taste*, can be found through Back2Print Publishing of Chicago. [blastfortune.com] [page 81]

Noel King
[Tralee, Co. Kerry, Ireland] has published more than a thousand poems, haiku, or short stories in magazines and journals in 38 countries. His poetry collections are: *Prophesying the Past* (2010), *The Stern Wave* (2013), and *Sons* (2015). [noelking.ie] [pages 10, 53, 77, 101, 108]

Marie Lecrivain
[Los Angeles, California] is the editor-publisher of *The Whiteside Review: A Journal of Speculative / Science Fiction*, a photographer, and writer-in-residence at her apartment. She's the author of several volumes of poetry and fiction, including *Grimm Conversations* (Sybaritic Press), and has been published in many print and online journals. [f: marieclecrivainauthor] [pages 12, 86, 116]

Jennifer Leeper
[Kansas City, Missouri] is an award-winning author of short and long works of fiction. Her long fiction includes *Padre*, a novella published by J. Burrage Publications, and *Padre: The Narrowing Path* and *Border Run and Other Stories*, both published by Barking Rain Press. Her publication credits include *Independent Ink Magazine*, *Every Day Fiction*, *Aphelion Webzine*, *Heater Magazine*, *Cowboy Jamboree*, *The New Engagement*, *Alaska Quarterly Review*, and *The Liguorian*. [t: @jenleeper1] [page 110]

Lyn Lifshin
[Arlington, Virginia] has published over 130 books and chapbooks, including three from Black Sparrow Press: *Cold Comfort*, *Before It's Light*, and *Another Woman Who Looks Like Me*. Recent books include: *A Girl Goes into the Woods* (NYQ Books), *For the Roses*, *Secretariat: The Red Freak*, *Tangled as the Alphabet: The Istanbul Poems*, *The Miracle*, *Malala*, *The Marilyn Poems*, and *Moving through Stained Glass: the Maple Poems*. Lyn was also the subject of a recent documentary, *Lyn Lifshin: Not Made of Glass*. [lynlifshin.com] [pages 9, 62, 104, 129]

Normal
[Saugerties, New York] remains "one of the last American primitives" in the underground press, with presently 600 pieces published between 1992

and 2019 (without the Internet). His most recent book, *I See Hunger's Children: Selected Poems 1962–2012*, was published by Lummox Press. [pages 11, 76, 95]

Jason Ryberg
[Kansas City, Missouri] is the author of seven books of poetry, six screenplays, and a few short stories. He was recently an artist-in-residence at the Prospero Institute of Disquieted Poetics and is an aspiring B-movie actor. His latest collection of poems is *Down, Down, and Away*, coauthored with Josh Rizer and released by Spartan Press. He lives with a rooster named Little Red and a billy goat named Giuseppe. [jasonryberg.blogspot.com] [pages 78, 114]

Victor Schwartzman
[Vancouver, Canada] has written since he was eight, majored in it at college, and continues writing today. He rarely submits. Early on there were a lot of rejections, although in the last 10 years, he's had better luck. Being published is nice, but it is dessert—it ain't the main course. [is.gd/VictorSchwartzman] [pages 18, 68, 94, 118]

The Poet Spiel
[Pueblo West, Colorado] has been internationally published. A lifetime of mental illness and decades of psychotherapy provide rich material for this author to work with. Born in 1941, confounded by loss associated with vascular dementia, Spiel struggles to keep his lips above desolation. [thepoetspiel.name] [page 119]

Alex Stolis
[Minneapolis, Minnesota] has had poems published in numerous journals. He is the author of *Justice for All* (Conversation Paperpress), a chapbook based on the last words of Texas Death Row inmates, and *A Cabal of Angels* (Red Bird Chapbooks), a collaborative chapbook with artist Susan Solomon. An e-chapbook, *From an iPod found in Canal Park; Duluth, MN*, was also released by Right Hand Pointing. He has been the recipient of five Pushcart nominations. [pages 15, 92, 109, 128]

David L. Tickel
[Morrisville, Pennsylvania] has had poems and stories appear in *Barbaric Yawp*, *Yalobusha Review*, *Hawaii Review*, *Happy*, *Nerve Cowboy*, *Hazmat*, *Trajectory*, *Front Window*, and *Transcendent Visions*. He paints houses for a living. [pages 54, 82, 112]

Acknowledgments

A very special thank you goes out to our Kickstarter donors, without whom this issue simply would not exist. Thank you, especially, to these precious few literary rockstars whose donations of $100 or greater fueled this final issue: Elaine Angstman, The Camel Saloon, Craig Desjardins, Daniel Harrison, Aaron Herfurth, Jeremy Laszlo, Dennis & Marta Litos, Out of Print, Charles P. Ries, Victor Schwartzman, Justin V. Smith, Debbie Soper, and Victoria Terry. Here's lookin' at you, kids.

Alternating Current wishes to acknowledge the following publications where pieces from issue No. 7 first appeared: "Spring Training" was previously published in *Art:Mag #36-A*. "The Mousehouse" was the winner of the SFSU Creative Writing Department's Marc Linenthal Award and was published in *Transfer*, Winter 2012, and in *Reverie: Ultra Short Memoirs* (Telling Our Stories Press, 2013). "Girls Are Cats and Guys Are Dogs" and "Lost and Found" were previously published by The Camel Saloon. "Homo erectus" was previously published in *Denver Syntax #17*. "Four voices at a high school graduation" was previously published in *Zygote in My Coffee*. "October" was previously published in *The Puffin Review*. "How My SUV Helped Me" was previously published in *Red Fez*. "No Words Required" was previously published in *Shemom #31* and *Westward Quarterly*, Winter 2009. "Softly and tenderly home: a trilogy" was previously published in *ZYX #63*. "The Photographer" was previously published in *Body of Work* (Formite Press, 2013).

Colophon

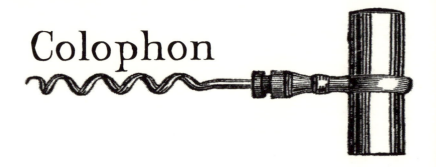

The edition you are holding is the First Print Edition of this publication.

Our *Poiesis Review* logo is set in The King & Queen Font, created by Bran, and in Mary Jane Larabie, created by Apostrophic Labs. The "7" and non-standard text of the title pages and cover, all interior title fonts, the biography name headers, and the drop capitals are set in Mary Jane Larabie. The back cover Alternating Current Press font is set in Portmanteau, created by JLH Fonts. All other fonts are set in Calisto MT. All fonts are used with permission; all rights reserved.

The tooth powder graphic on the title page and the corkscrew graphic in the title headers are in the public domain, courtesy of The Graphics Fairy. The scrollwork section dividers are from the Old Retro Labels TFB collection, created by Kaiser Zharkhan / Zanatlija. The Alternating Current lightbulb logo was created by Leah Angstman, ©2013, 2019 Alternating Current. The QR codes were created with QR Droid. To read QR codes on your smartphone, we recommend downloading QR Droid for Android or Zapper for iPhone. All graphics are used with permission; all rights reserved.

Front cover artwork: "It Feels Like Rain." Artwork by Loui Jover. Property of and ©2019 Loui Jover. Used with permission; all rights reserved. Find him at saatchiart.com/louijover, facebook.com/lojoverart, and Instagram at @louijover.

The editors wish to thank the font and graphic creators for allowing legal use.

Other Works from
Alternating Current Press

All of these books (and more) are available at Alternating Current's website: press.alternatingcurrentarts.com.

alternatingcurrentarts.com

Made in the USA
Middletown, DE
07 May 2019